D1299283

Awakening Your
Goddess

BARRON'S

Awakening Your
Goddess

3

A practical guide to discovering
a woman's power, a woman's glory

Liz Simpson

BARRON'S

First edition for the United States, its territories and possessions, and Canada
published by Barron's Educational Series, Inc., 2001.

Copyright © 2001 Gaia Books Ltd, London
Text copyright © 2001 Liz Simpson

The right of Liz Simpson to be identified as the author of this
work has been asserted in accordance with Sections 77 and 78
of the Copyright, Designs and Patents Act

All rights reserved.
No part of this book may be reproduced in any form, by photostat,
microfilm, xerography, or any other means, or incorporated into any
information retrieval system, electronic or mechanical, without the
written permission of the copyright owner.

First published in the United Kingdom in 2001 by Gaia Books Ltd,
66 Charlotte Street, London W1T 4QE, and
20 High Street, Stroud, Gloucestershire GL5 1AZ

All inquiries should be addressed to:
Barron's Educational Series, Inc.
250 Wireless Boulevard
Hauppauge, NY 11788
http://www.barronseduc.com

International Standard Book Number: 0-7641-1647-9
Library of Congress Catalog Card No. 2001086496

AL BR
BL473.5
.S56
2001

A GAIA ORIGINAL
Books from Gaia celebrate the vision of Gaia, the self-sustaining
living Earth, and seek to help readers live in greater personal and
planetary harmony.

Editor	Jo Godfrey Wood
Designer	Sara Mathews
Illustrator	Nanette Hoogslag
Managing Editor	Pip Morgan
Production	Lyn Kirby
Direction	Patrick Nugent

Printed and bound in Singapore by Imago

9 8 7 6 5 4 3 2 1

Holy Goddess Tellus,

Mother of Living Nature,

The food of life

Thou metest out of all eternal loyalty

And, when life has left us,

We take our refuge in Thee.

Thus everything Thou dolest out

Returns into Thy womb.

Rightly Thou art called Mother of the Gods

Because by Thy loyalty

Thou hast conquered the power of the Gods.

Verily Thou art also the Mother

Of the peoples and the Gods,

Without Thee nothing can thrive nor be;

Thou art powerful, of the Gods Thou art

The Queen and also the Goddess.

Thee, Goddess, and Thy power I now invoke;

Thou canst easily grant all that I ask

And in exchange I will give Thee,

Goddess, sincere thanks.

Eulogy, 2nd century A.D.

contents

introduction 8

introduction

Human beings tell stories. We tell stories to our children, not only when we read them the tales of Aesop or Grimm but when we talk about Santa Claus or the Tooth Fairy. We tell tales to friends and colleagues, enhancing the positive to show ourselves in the best possible light. Indeed, throughout life we construct a dynamic narrative for ourselves, modifying "reality" with the benefit of hindsight, new wisdom, and sometimes denial. Even twenty-first-century businesses use stories to help unpack organizational culture so that employees understand more effectively "how things are done around here." And corporate trainers increasingly use the power of narrative to unleash innate creativity, which today's businesses are so desperate to tap into. Why do we do this? Because stories engage our emotions and bring the underlying message alive in our hearts as well as our minds. As any teacher knows, enticing tales imbued with the capacity to awaken our imaginations and senses remain powerfully embedded in our memories long after they were first related. That is why such great sages as Christ, Lao Tzu, and Buddha created mental pictures by telling stories called parables. They wanted to ensure that the wisdom they imparted would be remembered and accurately passed on to the next generation.

You are about to enter the magical, mysterious world of another kind of symbolic storytelling – mythology. Like Christ's parables, stories about the exploits of gods, goddesses, and superheroes, such as Perseus and Hercules, were not passed on merely to entertain us. They contain universal truths about what it means to be human, transcending time and culture, so that they are as valid today as they were all those thousands of years ago. It was through their ability to relate to stories that our ancestors made sense of the world – stories about gods, goddesses, and heroes, embodying human traits and emotions – helping our ancestors to explore major philosophical questions such as, "Why are we here?" These stories also assisted our understanding about natural phenomena such as thunder and lightning, for which humans at that time had no rational explanation. The same anthropomorphism was applied to abstract concepts. For example, both ancient Greek and Norse societies explained the concept of fate in terms of Triple Goddesses, collectively known within the relevant traditions as the Moirae and the Norns (see also p. 27).

Goddess of today Each woman has the potential, power, and freedom to become her own Goddess, in her own way. We can draw on familiar ancient myths and legends for inspiration and insight, either accepting or rejecting their messages, as we see fit.

These goddesses were believed to spin humankind's destiny in the same way that their human counterparts spun cloth.

Mythology was also used politically, crafted by "spin doctors" of the day to promote the predominant ideology of their masters. As explained in Chapter One (see pp.16–27), myths are dynamic scripts, modified for the prevailing culture. Spin doctoring is not just a late twentieth-century phenomenon. Consider the different portrayals of Christ according to the varying focuses of the four Gospel writers. Matthew, Mark, Luke, and John presented strikingly varied versions of the same events because they each had their own, very different, perspective of Christ's life.

Several thousand years ago as largely peaceful, art-loving, "matrifocal" societies, such as ancient Crete, were overrun by aggressive, warlike peoples, so the stories created about the meaning and purpose of human existence changed to promote the new patriarchal values. Mythology runs counter to what the Bible tells us. Through these stories our ancestors created gods in their own image. In Hindu mythology this was literally the case, whereby Mahadevi, the Great Goddess, was said to have formed the Universe from her own body – the oceans her bowels, the mountains her bones, and the trees her hair. As Nietzsche said, in Greek culture the gods "justified life by living it."

Unfortunately, the term "myth" has become synonymous with factual inaccuracy or misunderstanding, but nothing is further from the truth. The word itself comes from the Greek *mythos*, meaning story. Mythology should not be mistaken for legend, folklore, or the religious model on which the monotheistic faiths are based. Mythology links the mortal and immortal worlds – in metaphorical terms, the conscious and unconscious realms of our minds. Indeed, it is a true religion in the sense that it accomplishes the original meaning of the word *religio*, to rebind.

The dramatis personae of mythology represent a rich source of archetypes or patterns of personality. By recognizing the different dispositions – positive and dysfunctional – we can gain insights into how to overcome more effectively the mental, emotional, and spiritual challenges that we each face as we journey from birth to death. More importantly, archetypes help us bring into consciousness those aspects of our personality whose existence we may be repressing.

Through our appreciation of the underlying messages of myths we are in a better position to piece back together the fragmentation of the human soul that has taken place over many thousands of years.

Mythology may be as traditional a form of narrative as legend, but unlike their legendary counterparts, for example, King Arthur and Robin Hood, who were thought to have been real people, mythological characters are fictitious. Their timeless quality and power does necessitate a historical setting. And while folklore is concerned with the common practices, beliefs, and superstitions of a particular culture, mythology is more a "living faith," characterizing storytellers' views on major issues such as birth, death, afterlife, and immortality. Or, as historian Mircea Eliade explains, myths help to "light the deepest aspects of reality which defy any other means of knowledge." A myth is a form of sacred symbolism in which readers can glean meaning about themselves. Each one is a fantastic story of derring-do, recounting adventures, but scratching the surface, and beneath superficial layers of a thrilling tale is a highly sophisticated set of psychological resources to help us explore different, more empowering, ways to think, feel, and behave. Hidden in the imagery and drama describing the ritualistic transformation of a superhuman being are clues about how we can live more balanced, joyous, and fulfilled lives through recognizing, accepting, or modifying common emotional patterns.

One of the key themes of this book is the importance of balancing all aspects of our intrinsic nature, so that we joyously rediscover feminine principles subsumed by the supremacy of male gods such as Zeus and, in later cultures, the misogynous monotheism of Christianity, Judaism, and Islam. This applies to each one of us, male or female. One aim of this book, in its focus on the Goddess, or female archetype, is simply to redress the balance stemming from thousands of

years of male cultural dominance. The purpose here is not to replace one set of approaches with another, but to integrate masculine and feminine principles in a way that enhances all our lives. Another principal focus is to help bring about acceptance of the ambiguities of the human experience, allowing us to get in touch with our Shadow side as well as more favorable aspects. In this way we acknowledge and respect the Higher Self as well as the demanding Ego, the sinner and the saint, the divine and the diabolical. Why is this important? Because only when we fully accept ourselves – "warts and all" – can we become compassionate, forgiving, and nonjudgmental toward all those around us.

In many ways these ancient tales of the deeds of the gods and other beings are very similar to today's scientific explanations of universal phenomena. Despite lacking the benefit of computer simulations and other technological tools, our ancestral storytellers came up with some remarkably similar interpretations concerning humankind's most perplexing questions, such as, "How was the Universe created?" and "How did life on Earth begin?" Apart from the simplicity of our ancestors' explanations and lack of a specified time frame, both science and mythology share an inability to explain precisely what happened to trigger the creation of the Universe. Whereas there is a tendency to set great store by "facts" as presented by scientists, some of the greatest scientific discoveries have, actually, been powered by the imagination. The early exponents of the Big Bang theory did not formulate it through observational evidence, the accepted criteria upon which science is based. Like Darwin's Origin of the Species, Einstein's Theory of Relativity, and German chemist Kekule's discovery of the structure of the benzene molecule, it was originally "dreamed up."

The purpose of this book is to help you better understand some of the unconscious forces influencing your attitudes, beliefs, and behavior, through exploring the archetypes illustrated by fifteen Goddesses from a selection of cultures. In Chapter Two I suggest the most effective ways of using the material found in subsequent sections. This involves, in particular, exploring who you believe your Self to be and whether its facets are helping or hindering you from living the life you want, according to the relationships you have with your significant other, your family, and your Self. This self-exploratory work is pulled together in Chapter Six, which focuses on integrating or mediating the various archetypes according to what you most need in your life. In addition to the tools and techniques outlined in this book, particularly within the Goddess spreads found in Chapters Three, Four, and Five, another key theme surfaces: how much our thoughts, attitudes, and behavior have become distorted by the patriarchal ideology into which we have been immersed since birth.

In the chapter that follows, in which we explore the historical fall and rise of the Goddess, we discover how "patrifocal" dualism – the notion of right versus wrong, good versus evil, Us versus Them – has polarized humanity in the most disastrous way. Unwilling to accept that male and female are complementary, patriarchal societies have systematically denigrated such qualities as nurturing, compassion, feminine intuition, motherhood, and mediation. It can seem like a no-win situation for women, since those who display the same focus, determination, and forthrightness as men are derided as being less than feminine. It sometimes seems that women are prized only for physical allure and sexuality – and when those go....

A telling example of definitions of female worth is described in the story of the Judgment of Paris, written for a patriarchal audience of ancient Greece, and whose outcome was eventually to lead to the Trojan Wars. This mythological tale also helps to introduce the theme of the Triple Goddess (see pp. 26–27). As revenge for not being invited to the wedding of Peleus, King of Thessaly, to the sea nymph, Thetis, the Goddess of Strife, Eris, sent along to the ensuing festivities a present of a golden apple. This prize was to be given to the fairest and most beautiful goddess among the many that inhabited Olympia. Hera, Athena, and Aphrodite all claimed that the apple belonged to them. The chief of the gods, Zeus, realizing that the decision would cause havoc among these three strong-willed, proud goddesses decided that a mortal, handsome Paris, should choose which one of them was to be awarded the gift.

Each goddess, after agreeing to abide by Paris' decision, took part in the divine equivalent of a Miss Universe contest, their aim being to influence his vote. First came Hera, Goddess of Marriage and wife of Zeus – the mother figure in this triplicity of goddesses. She offered him power, saying that she would make him Lord of Asia and rich beyond his wildest dreams if he chose her. Athena, the Greek Warrior Goddess, came next. Renowned as a superlative strategist and representing the Maiden or Virgin, she promised Paris victory in all his battles and wisdom to benefit from such power. Finally, Aphrodite, Goddess of Love and Beauty, who stunned the youthful Paris with her seduction technique, offered to give him the most beautiful, passionate woman in the world – Helen, wife of King Menelaus. Aphrodite represents another facet within the Triple Goddess theme – not the Wise Woman, Widow, or Crone, but the Whore. Paris, allowing lust to cloud his mind, decreed Aphrodite the winner and, after abducting Helen, sparked the Trojan War.

The message is clear: What mortal men respond to is not riches or power, wisdom, or superiority in battle, but sex and physical beauty. As such they downgrade – sometimes fail even to acknowledge – the other gifts that women can offer. At least the storyteller had the good grace to point out the disastrous consequences that come about when one factor within the Goddess Triplicity is elevated above all others. Given such propaganda, which has been promoted within patriarchal cultures for around 3,000 years, is it any wonder that women are raised to pay less attention to personal qualities and interpersonal skills than they do to making themselves look attractive?

The Goddess, in her various guises of Maiden, Mother, and Wise Woman, sister, wife, and widow, or light, shadow, and mediating force, offers a new, more empowering, perspective. Ask how much of your intrinsic nature you perceive as unimportant, of no value, as negative, or "dark," and thus seek to suppress it. Ancient Chinese wisdom teaches us that life, according to the concept of Yin and Yang, is comprised of complementary polarities. We cannot know true joy without experiencing sorrow; we could not appreciate the light without knowing the dark, and without sunshine and rain we could never delight in a rainbow.

MALE
Hierarchy
Competition
Domination over nature
Divine as external, separate from Self
Fear and persecution of "the Other"
Dualism – black versus white
Management
Profit
Expert medical knowledge
Outer power
Separation from the whole
External focus prompting distrust

If you look at the interpretation of the Yin–Yang symbol below you will see how each side contains an element of the other. Each of us, regardless of gender, has both masculine or feminine in our makeup. Therefore we must all reconnect with the Goddess within. Why is this important? Consider for a moment what "power" means to the extremely patriarchally focused mind as experienced during the Spanish Inquisition, the witch-hunts of the Middle Ages, and in many male-dominated businesses today, and compare that with archetypal feminine qualities.

He had taught me how to cast a fishing lure, how to pee into a toilet, and how to pound a nail. But he had not taught me how to speak from the heart. After 3,000 years of patriarchy and focus on masculine values, in which the feminine within each of us has been fractured and split from the whole, this quotation is a sad indictment. It illustrates an era in which we have seen the escalation of a scientific world view that has tried to suppress concepts that cannot be proven, including love and the existence of a Higher Power. If we concern ourselves only with facts then we are denying the value of those characteristics traditionally associated with the feminine and thus the complete experience of being human. Generally, we learn emotional matters – how to operate from the heart – from our mothers. If we deny the Great Mother or Goddess archetype, then our existence has less meaning than a robot's. To awaken the Goddess we must come out of our heads and venture into our hearts. The purpose of this book, whether you are male or female, is to help you reconnect to the feminine, the Shadow, and your Divine nature. I am honored to guide you through this beneficial and transformative experience. *Enjoy!*

FEMALE
Equality
Consultation
Nurturing, caring, environmentalism
Divine within, integrated with Self
Acceptance of diversity
Richer, multihued viewpoints
Mentoring and coaching
Corporate social responsibility
Self-healing
Inner power
Universal connectedness
Introspection leading to transformation

history of the goddess

1

Once upon a time God was a goddess. When you consider that our ancestors created divinities in their own image, giving them human characteristics according to the dominant culture, this is understandable. Both biological and archaeological evidence suggests that early social development evolved around the female. The male was not considered fundamental either to mother or child and male contact with offspring was precarious. Long before monogamy and marriage were devised, a woman might be impregnated by several men, any of whom might be the father of the child. Before and even after the establishment of settled communities during the Neolithic period mother and child would expect little contact with the father. So both childbearing and nurturing, the responsibility of the woman, required females to take charge of producing food. When agriculture replaced hunting, women became landowners. Thus, the earliest economic and social power was matriarchal.

Women are now credited by pre-historians as being the catalysts in the spread of this new way – promoting the very concept of culture. The female archetypes of creation and destruction were thereafter linked with the Earth, on which communities relied. When the Earth was fertile, people lived; when it was barren, they died.

Images of Earth goddesses: At the earliest-known urban center, Catal Huyuk (c.7200–6500 B.C.E.), archaeologists have documented a plethora of images and symbols of voluptuous Earth goddesses. Prior to cases being made by archaeologists such as Marija Gimbutas, historian Gerda Lerner, and author Merlin Stone that communities such as Catal Huyuk seemed to be inhabited by peace-loving, creative individuals acceding to a matriarchate, other voices have raised objections. Few of us see ancient artifacts objectively, imbuing them with contemporary meanings that may have no basis in fact. Thus, many historians have shown discomfort with the notion of Goddess culture by questioning whether any greater value was really placed on female attributes in prehistoric times. This may be true, but let us examine some of the other evidence indicating the importance of the feminine at this time. Excavation of Iron Age tombs in northern Europe suggests that women were interred with great ceremony, accompanied by valuable goods, implying high social status. We know of female Celtic rulers, such as the Icenean warrior queen, Boudicca, and the Battle Goddesses, the Morrigan (see p. 27), played an important role in the wars of Celtic peoples. Known as shape shifters, the Morrigan were associated with ravens or crows. If one of these harbingers of death was seen on the battlefield, this was enough to signal impending disaster. In ancient Egypt, prior to its unification into a single state and the emergence of the concept of Divine Kingship, families would trace their line through the mother's side. Ancient Chinese writings refer to Tibet as "the land of women" and Japan as "the land of queens," and women in ancient Crete assumed prominent roles as hunters, bull-leapers, artisans, potters, and weavers. Figures on frescos show men as smaller than the central female figure – probably the Goddess or High Priestess.

The earliest mythological tales place emphasis on a female Creatrix, usually giving birth to a male partner with whom she would mate to produce offspring. Divine male consorts were neither deemed superior nor equal to the Mother, but were considered necessary only to impregnate the female. In early Saxon times the word "husband" was merely the man who tended to the woman's property, since until Christianity, property rights among ancient British tribes were passed through the female line.

So how did the concept of an all-powerful Earth Goddess become subsumed by a male-dominated pantheon? Although the exact time frame is sketchy, it is believed that between 4000 and 3500 B.C.E. a combination of races, Indo-Europeans, emerged from the steppes of Asia Minor, migrated south and west into Old Europe, bringing with them a new culture, a new form of economic exchange, and new ideology: patriarchy. These warlike peoples transformed the social fabric of the cultures they overran and replaced matriarchal religious authority with male political power. This small ruling elite, whose wealth lay in horses and metals rather than land, glorified masculinity because it produced combative males, thus, military success. Their gods were warriors, headed by a sky divinity later known as Zeus. The land-loving Neolithic communities, led by women whose use of metals was confined to tools and ornaments, were no match for invaders such as the Kurgans from the Black Sea, who could produce lethal weapons.

In the same way that later the Christian Church absorbed pagan festivals in order to attempt to obliterate the "Old Religion," the Goddess motif was integrated into the new patriarchal pantheon. The new regime could not only invade a woman's body through rape but set about usurping female power over the land by disseminating stories about the relationship between men and women. Through manipulating existing narratives, the new male-dominated rule justified their treatment of women with tales in which the promiscuous Zeus cheated on his queen, the goddess Hera, and raped nymphs, mortal women, and minor deities. What better way could this small ruling elite assert their ultimate power than through the glorification of patriarchy? Here are some examples of how older tales about the power of the Goddess were adapted to suit the new ideology.

Before the barbarous hunters, the Dorians, invaded Greece, bringing with them the Sky God Zeus, the indigenous peoples honored the Great Goddess. She not only presided over the fertile Earth but controlled the Heavens and ruled the Underworld. Hence the sacred feminine is regarded as both the giver of life and the bringer of death. One of the symbols associated with this supreme female deity was a cow called Rhea, whose alter ego may have been the goddess Hera – literally "the Earth." Since the cult of Hera predated that of Zeus, many temples existed to worship her exclusively. However, if you are planning to successfully co-opt a strong, existing religion into a new regime, what better way to do it than to divide and conquer? Unlike the early Israelites, who insisted that theirs (Yahweh) was the only God, the Indo-European invaders took a more insidious approach. Over time the concept of the Great Mother was fragmented and subsumed into the Greek pantheon, taking on a variety of roles and guises, one of which was Hera. The classification of Greek gods and goddesses was an afterthought, being first presented in Hesiod's *Theogony*, written around 800 B.C.E., although the Mother cult of Hera is believed to be significantly older. The earlier goddess undoubtedly bore little resemblance to the patriarchally modified consort, who time after time was humiliated and hurt by her husband. What is important about the marriage of Zeus and Hera is that it signifies the uneasy merging of the patriarchal invaders with the indigenous matriarchy. As you will discover in Hera's story (see p. 84), the Great Goddess was reduced to the stereotype of a jealous, vindictive wife. In order to diminish and weaken her power, the activities of the "father of gods and men" turned his wife into a laughingstock, thereby reducing her power in the eyes of the populace.

In keeping with the nature of myths in mirroring human experience, it has been suggested that this unhappy union represented the loveless state of marriage at that time. This is not surprising when you consider that many involved the forcible merging of two very different cultures. The story of Zeus and Hera also highlights the psychological challenges that warriors would have

when required to settle into peaceful domesticity, since Zeus is portrayed as a wife abuser and Hera his battered consort. One of the negative aspects of the Hera archetype is the unwillingness to direct anger at the perpetrator of shame and hurt. In Hera's case her rage and vindictiveness were not directed at her husband but at the various women he seduced and the children he sired.

It is interesting to note how later male storytellers changed the original narratives to better fit the new ideology. Demeter and Persephone's remote origins show them to be the Grain Mother and her maiden daughter (see pp. 78–83 and 56–61). Their story forms the basis of the Eleusinian mysteries. Despite being a religious practice open to all, Greek or foreigner, the war-like newcomers to Greece would have been precluded from the initiation rites, since the requirements included not having taken a human life. Although the story was not written down until Homer's *Hymn to Demeter*, c.700 B.C.E., reference to Persephone's entry into the Underworld appears on Minoan artifacts from 2000 B.C.E. on, during which time it would have passed on in the oral tradition. The pre-Hellenic myth is different from the later Homeric version in significant ways. According to the matriarchal rendition of the myth, the maiden willingly enters the Underworld, neither abducted nor raped by Hades. In this version Persephone meets distressed spirits of the dead as she wanders over the hills collecting flowers. Concerned that they might have no one to guide or watch over them, she speaks to her mother. The older goddess replies that it is her function to care for these spirits, but that she has had to neglect

that duty in order to concentrate on tending the crops. Persephone then offers to take on that role herself, and despite Demeter's attempts to dissuade her, the maiden enters the lower domain, depicted on early pottery as an open vagina.

Within the deep chasm of the Earth, Persephone calls each of the spirits to her and marks their foreheads with pomegranate juice, an initiatory gesture enabling them to be reborn into the upper world. Demeter mourns the loss of her beloved daughter, neglecting her earthly responsibilities. Only when she notices a crocus blooming in spring, is Demeter reunited with her daughter. The mother is then forced to accept that, for part of the year, her maiden alter ego must descend into the Underworld to comfort and guide the spirits of the dead, enabling them to achieve their next incarnation. What is interesting to note in both of these Greek myths is that the new rulers did not allow their misogyny to completely override their intelligence. They did have the good grace to recognize that women have power over men. Even almighty Zeus had to concede that Demeter had the power to destroy humankind through failing to cause crops to grow, and was thereby forced, according to the later story, to allow Persephone's return, at least for part of the year.

Arguably it has been the Catholic Church that has been the greatest enemy of women and Goddess culture over the centuries. Its ways were even more subtle than those of the Indo-European warlords as it sought to eradicate paganism by adopting its symbolism and incorporating its festivals into the Christian calendar. One such example is the story of Saint Brigit, originally an ancient Celtic Triple Goddess (see pp. 26–27), venerated throughout the northern European empire known as Brigantia. Brigit governed healing, fertility, poetry, and smithcraft in an age when female knowledge and innate skills were revered, and underpinned cultures based on matriarchal values. The cult of Brigit was so strongly embedded in Ireland that the Catholic Church reinvented the goddess as a nun. Even the concept of the pagan trinity was Christianized into Brigit, her son, Saint Patrick, and the maiden martyr, Saint Columba, the Holy Dove. The pagan festival of Brigit on the first of February, celebrating the arrival of spring, was renamed Candlemas by the Church and this Celtic goddess was canonized.

The Church borrowed extensively from older goddess myths and the Bible contains many such sources, some only minor deviations from the pool of universal archetypes, but with an obvious antipagan slant. For example, the Hebrew portrayal of Adam's first wife, Lilith, was an incorporation of the Sumero–Babylonian Creation Goddess known variously as Belili, Baalat, Astarte, or Eostre (root of the word Easter).

Before the days in which male-dominant societies subjugated women and the Roman Catholic Church determined sex evil and paganistic, matriarchal societies freely combined religion and sex. The union of men and women was closer to Eastern approaches, such as tantric sex, with emphasis on sensuality and quality of experience. Lilith, in keeping with other sexually liberated goddesses, represented this equality of sexual expression. Unwilling to suppress her joy of sex and thinking of herself as Adam's equal, Lilith was thought to represent antipatriarchal values and thus was first turned into a figure of evil and eventually written out of the canonical Bible. She was replaced by Eve, a more subservient helpmate to Adam.

Eve is linked with the serpent, an early totemic form of the Great Goddess associated with immortality and the active female energy flowing through the Earth. In keeping with the defamation of women's innate powers and because of the Indo-European warlords' fear of female spirituality, Eve and the serpent became scapegoats for mankind's banishment from paradise, further undermining women. The earlier myth, whereby Lilith was made from dust, was further distorted to strengthen the new male-oriented psychology. Thus, in the later story, God created Eve from

Adam's rib, to be his companion. Throughout matriarchal cultures the female divinity, not the male, was considered the Creatrix.

Another myth that illustrates the collision of the two ideologies of matriarchy and patriarchy is the Epic of Gilgamesh, whose core theme is achieving immortality. This Assyro–Babylonian poem, written c.700 B.C.E., undoubtedly influenced early Jewish writers of the Bible. Its characters include a serpent, a woman who "robs" the hero Enkidu of his innocence (Adam in the Garden of Eden), a flood hero (Noah), and precognitive dreams (Joseph advising the Pharaoh in Egypt).

According to the story, Gilgamesh is approached by the Goddess Ishtar, who desires him as her husband. Gilgamesh calls her a harlot, refusing her advances, apparently because he is aware that she discards lovers when they cease to please. However, the male Indo-European mind would undoubtedly have associated Ishtar with the rites carried out by her priestesses, in which bulls were emasculated and their severed genitals offered in honour of the Goddess. Also, the sacred lovemaking and sexual-spiritual joyfulness that honor the female approach is about surrendering the ego, a concept with which the new patriarchal ideology would have been very uncomfortable. As revenge for being shunned Ishtar strikes down Gilgamesh's friend, Enkidu, with a fatal illness. If there is one sure way to subjugate women universally, it is by demonizing them, thus creating fear and mistrust between the sexes and offering justification for one's persecution over the other.

Most books written to help us explore and heal fractures caused by the subjugation of the sacred female focus on ancient Greek goddesses. This is said to be because Greek characters and mythic themes are more commonly known through the arts and literature. My aim is to broaden this focus, so you will find references to goddesses from Celtic, Chinese, Egyptian, and Norse cultures as well as the Greek. While there is similarity between the myths of cultures separated by space and time, there are also some differences of which I think it is worth being aware. It is important not to regard matriarchy as patriarchy, but with the other sex in control. Robert Brifault, writing in *The Mothers* (1927), asserted that in primitive matriarchal societies women did not dominate men but simply exerted their natural authority based on enhanced interpersonal skills and empathy with the land; thus, women were the innovators of culture. It may seem almost impossible to believe that such female authority once existed. Patriarchal mythology is far easier to accept because it illustrates life as we recognize it, with men desiring control and women regarded as resources. The paternalistic monotheistic religions of Christianity, Islam, and Judaism have played a powerful role in belittling women through the ages. Wise women–the herbalists, midwives, and healers, who were in touch with their spiritual nature–were labeled "witches." Because of the fear this induced in male-dominated culture, which did not understand that communing with Nature is a natural gift, females were persecuted mercilessly through the ages.

Patriarchy has not always been the natural order; it is just that men – and women – conspire to maintain the status quo. But if we truly want to reconnect with the Goddess and heal the psychological and spiritual fracture that prevents us from knowing our whole selves, then things must, and can, change. It did those thousands of years ago when patriarchy replaced a "matrifocal" view of life, and can change again today. We just need to start rewriting the stories, beginning with our personal narratives.

Ceridwen, Keeper of the Cauldron of Inspiration and Knowledge, was a mythical Welsh sorceress who used shape-shifting to wield her power (see also pp. 114–115).

the triple goddess

The number three has long been considered special. The sixth-century B.C.E. ancient Greek philosopher and mathematician, Pythagoras, called it "the perfect number," saying that three was the expression of beginning, middle, and end, and therefore a symbol of divinity. Indeed, the threefold godhead emerges in great religions from Christianity (Father, Son, Holy Spirit) to Hinduism (Brahma, Vishnu, Shiva). Ancient Norse cultures revered the triumvirate of Odin, Frigg, and Balder, while in ancient Egypt it was Osiris, Isis, and Horus. In classical Roman mythology, power was considered to rest in the hands of Jupiter (Heavens), Neptune (seas), and Pluto (Underworld).

The trinity is a motif that runs through all sorts of phenomena, symbolizing something that is the sum of one (single focus) and two (duality). We have three primary colors – red, blue, and yellow – from which all other colors are mixed. The guilds had a three-step process—apprentice, fellow, and master—and Christ talked about the way, the truth, and the life. In folktales it is common for the witch or fairy godmother to facilitate three wishes, with the third usually being required to overcome the difficulties that arose from foolishly wasting the first two.

In this book, goddesses are categorized according to the Maiden, Mother, and Wise Woman (or Crone) archetypes. But there are other ways of acknowledging the different energies and qualities of the archetypal feminine and you are invited to choose whichever feels right for you.

Threesomes Here are some examples of the tendency for things to be grouped in threes:
* Past, present, future
* Length, width, height
* Animal, vegetable, mineral
* Liquid, solid, gas
* Mass, power, velocity
* Air, water, earth
* Mind, body, spirit
* New, waxing, waning Moons
* Virgin, Mother, and Elder (or Crone)
* Child, bride, widow
* Creator, destroyer, and preserver/mediator
* Birth-giver, nurturer, and death-bringer

Traditional trinities Some mythologies illustrate the different aspects or energies of the divine feminine as a triad. For example,

The Vikings had the Norns – Norse goddesses of fate and spinners of destiny:
* Ur – past or waxing Moon
* Verdandi – present or full Moon
* Skuld – future or waning Moon
These correspond to the Greek Moirae, children of the Creation Goddess, Nyx:
* Clotho – the spinner
* Lachesis – the apportioner
* Atropos – the inevitable.

The ancient Celts of Ireland had the Morrigan, a triplicity of war, fertility, and vegetation goddesses:
* Morrigan – "phantom Queen"
* Badb – "the crow or Raven"
* Macha – "frenzy in battle"
The Morrigan not only represented the complementary generative and destructive characteristics of the sacred feminine but are also said to have expressed the harsh, unrelenting warrior nature of the Celtic soul.

The Furies were three crones within the very earliest Greek pantheon, who were said to live in Hades, or the Underworld, and whose mission it was to guard the matriarchal bloodline by avenging the murder of a mother by her son, as in the story of Clytemnestra and Orestes.
    Their names and attributes are:
* Alecto – anger
* Tisiphone – retaliation
* Megaera – jealousy
    Once patriarchal values had overturned the earlier matriarchal focus, the Furies were prettied up, renamed the Eumenides, and given gentler, less terrifying, dispositions.

In Hindu mythology the goddess metamorphosing into various aspects or primal energies is illustrated by Shiva's wife, Shakti. She is known variously as Parvati, the beautiful maiden, Uma, the devoted ascetic, and Durga, the invincible destroyer of demons. But she is perhaps best known and venerated as Kali Ma ("the black mother" – see pp. 98–103), whose conflicting personality represents the rebirth that follows destruction. Kali Ma is commonly depicted as full breasted and naked, blood dripping from her lips and nails. In this terrible manifestation she is a killer of demons.

Shakespeare worked the Goddess archetypes into his plays. We are probably most familiar with the three witches or crones in *Macbeth* and King Lear's three daughters:
* Goneril
* Regan
* Cordelia
    These could represent the ancient struggle between the new patriarchal order (in the guise of Lear himself) and the Triple Goddess. In this context, the story illustrates the disharmony that comes from dualism, when one facet of the Goddess – in this case, Cordelia – is denied.

accessing goddess wisdom

2

While it is important for any book to be both informative and inspiring, those in the self-help genre also need to be very practical. They need to outline ways to help you bring about desired changes in your current attitudes, beliefs, and behavior and thus your life as a whole. That is why you will find in these pages a plethora of tools and techniques that will bring Goddess knowledge to life for you. Some of these will appeal to you more than others, but I urge you to keep an open mind about all of them. We are often wary of experimenting with something that does not seem to be "my kind of thing." But when we are exploring new territory it helps to be as well prepared as possible. Please get involved with this book. You will undoubtedly get some benefit from reading about the goddesses and the vital role mythology and ritual have to play in all our lives. But it is only by setting aside private time to engage in the exercises, and really get under the skin of these archetypes, that significant change can take place. What we are aiming for is less intellectual appreciation of the Goddess archetypes, rather more of an emotional understanding. For that you need to bring

your heart and soul, as well as your mind, to this process. Before I go into detail about what you can expect in this book, let us look at the bigger picture. Which of these approaches – the intellectual/theoretical or the emotional/practical – you decide to take is up to you. If you simply want to read through this book and give some thought to how the Goddess archetypes are demonstrated in your life, you will undoubtedly gain a degree of value from that. However, if you really want to change your life, becoming truly fulfilled and complete, then I urge you to get into this book at a deeper level.

Each of the goddesses featured in Chapters Three, Four, and Five has been carefully chosen to highlight a common life issue in terms of your relationship with your Significant Other, your close family, and, most important, your relationship with yourself. Each of these Goddess myths will help you uncover those values, characteristics, and behavior that may not be benefiting you. Because they are so deeply embedded in your culture and upbringing, you may not be consciously aware of them. It is only by bringing subconscious issues into the light that you are able to confront and, if necessary, modify dysfunctional attitudes and behaviors. The great Swiss spiritual psychologist, Jung, considered the Goddess archetypes to be a potent force in the unconscious, likening them to "an inherited mode of psychic functioning," like a chick emerging from an egg. If you want to benefit from the positive qualities of the feminine principle, then you need to take an active role in expressing this in all areas of your life.

Finally, Chapter Six shows you how to pull all this self-knowledge together so that you can summon and channel the strengths of the various goddesses at any particular time in your life. This is especially important at those times when you find yourself facing a major life issue – for example, when you are committing to a partner, trying to achieve work–life balance, coming to terms with infidelity, or coping after your children have left home. In a sense this book represents the cycle of life. It challenges you to accept the death of old, outmoded ways of thinking and offers ways in which to bring about a rebirth of your Goddess within. This will stimulate greater personal growth and development and thus help you live the life you have always wanted.

Expressing the feminine principle

This book shows you how to express the feminine principle in all areas of your life, through:

∗ Presenting each Goddess story according to the psychological treasures that lie within these ancient narratives

∗ Highlighting both the dysfunctional and positive qualities associated with each archetype

∗ Offering you a series of self-exploratory questions with which you can more easily and quickly realign yourself with the Divine Feminine and therefore become the fulfilled person you have always known yourself to be

∗ Suggesting various ways in which you can develop your chosen Goddess archetype(s) through visualizations, affirmations, keeping a journal (see pp. 38–39), recognizing the importance of ritual (see p. 33), and altar creation (see pp. 36–37).

From reading this book you will gain:

∗ An introduction to the nature of the spiritual feminine and how the various archetypes affect our lives

∗ An overview of the fall and rise of matriarchal values

∗ Insight into a variety of cultures in which the Goddess has played a significant role

∗ An appreciation that to live a life of joyful fulfilment, each one of us needs to achieve balance, not just in terms of recognizing that male and female aspects are complementary, not in opposition, but also by actively engaging the influences that contribute to the Goddess as Maiden, Mother, and Wise Woman.

From working with this book you will gain:

∗ A means by which you will better recognize the different archetypes operating in your life at the moment and a series of tools and techniques with which to modify dysfunctional patterns and emphasize positive Goddess influences

∗ An understanding of how you can contribute to a new world paradigm – in which both male and female archetypes are honored and respected in equal measure for their joint contribution to the richness of human existence

∗ A way of recognizing how far your social conditioning informs your life, as well as the chance to assess the extent to which this is serving you

∗ An opportunity to critically appraise how balanced your life currently is, safe in the knowledge that you can achieve equilibrium and holism any time you choose.

Self-exploration is a key feature of each of the Goddess sections. In addition to the general questions posed at the end of this chapter and in Chapter Six, each Goddess narrative includes an opportunity for examining your attitudes and behavior with regard to the theme or issue being presented. The answers to these open questions are to be found within yourself. This book merely acts as a catalyst to help you excavate the wisdom of your soul. You have the right to live your life as you choose; any worthwhile self-help book should guide and support you rather than offer "answers" that, by their very nature, are highly prescriptive. A fundamental part of personal development work is taking responsibility for your life and that is what you are being coached to do here.

I passionately believe that within each of us lies the answer to every question that has ever been asked, is being asked, or will ever be asked. Our souls are the repositories of our Divinity and as such are conduits to Divine Knowledge. In order to tap into that wellspring of wisdom you are asked to set aside some quiet, contemplative time when you can ponder each of these questions in turn. Let the issues that each presents wash over you, without trying to force an answer. By allowing yourself to become deeply relaxed and focused on the breath, you will be able to harness your innate creativity, that always produces the right solution for you. In that way you will be able to feel, and not just think, the answers.

What you are aiming to tap into is the wisdom of your Higher Self and not the superficial focus of your ego, which dominates most of the time. This process cannot be rushed, however. Self-discovery is not an overnight affair, much to the dismay of those of us who love the "quick fix." Allow yourself to live with these questions for a short time.

It has been said that while myth provides the plot, ritual enables the experience. Each of us, no matter how much in control we think we are, must recognize that life is mutable – if not completely chaotic – at times. The way in which our ancestors learned to cope was by engaging in regularly repeated symbolic actions or behaviors that, by their very nature, provided them with a sense of security and confidence. Unfortunately, rituals have all but disappeared from our lives today. And the psychological consequences, including a near-global epidemic of depression, are great. Even sitting together for Sunday lunch has given way to a flurry of individual activities, fueling feelings of disconnection and separation. I encourage you to make ritual a part of your life as you begin to awaken your Goddess within. This can include making regular entries in your journal (see keeping a journal, pp. 38-39), revisiting your altar (see altar creation, pp. 36-37) on a weekly basis to review how you wish to change it, or visualizing yourself as your chosen Goddess while pampering yourself in the bath. In order for you to effectively work through the process of cultivating your Goddess energy, it is important to take small but consistent steps. Getting into the habit of allocating a time and place to your Goddess work – regardless of the degree of ceremony you choose to assign to it – helps to construct the psychological scaffolding with which you can better cope with all life's uncertainties.

If you want to cut a piece of wood, a screwdriver would be useless. Similarly, you would be unable to meet your objective to erect a perfectly horizontal shelf by employing an egg timer rather than a level. Each of us harbors a psychological toolbox of "archetypes." These are our preconscious dispositions with which we

react to particular challenges. That is to say, each of us is imprinted with a number of instinctual patterns of thought and behavior that manifest themselves at particular times in our lives. The archetypal pool from which our psychic selves have drawn to produce our personalities is universal, although our own blend of them is unique. Unfortunately, like the analogy above, we may find ourselves ill equipped to deal with the myriad of new requirements with which life confronts us. That is why it is important to identify which archetypes may need to be added to our psychological toolbox and which may need to be discarded.

That is not to fall into the trap of patriarchal dualism by labeling some of the tendencies "bad" and others "good." For example, one of the most basic of these potentials is the Shadow archetype. This represents the dark side of our natures that orthodox religious ideology has mythologized as Satan. We have been brainwashed into denying the Shadow. Because this is a part of the natural order of things and therefore cannot be totally eradicated, we project our Shadows on to others. Thus we believe that other people are the ones who are jealous, selfish, angry, uncompassionate – not us. Yet if we are honest with ourselves it is the very characteristics in others that irritate or anger us most that tend to be the traits we deny acknowledging within ourselves. Thus the biggest gossip may be outraged by the way other people gossip.

The early Goddess movement accepted the part that the Shadow has to play in life, understanding that, without it, none of us can ever be complete or whole. That is why Goddess-worshipping cultures were comfortable with the archetype of the Terrible Mother as well as the Good Mother, acknowledging the all-inclusive aspects of both the dark, vengeful, destructive Goddess as well as the light, supportive Creatrix. This is the undeniable synthesis of life and death.

Our ancestors recognized that this is how human existence is – a psychic interplay of many facets that later commentators chose to label "good" or "bad" (see also reference to Yin and Yang on pp. 14–15). Every archetypal pattern offers us opportunities, whether to experience joy or to learn a valuable lesson. Balancing your archetypes involves recognizing that their value lies in the extent to which they are helping you create the life you truly want and to use even those that seem undesirable as catalysts for insight, understanding, and growth. The interplay of so-called positives and negatives is wonderfully illustrated in many fairy tales. Like myths, they are a storehouse of psychological metaphor, beginning with a happy situation that suddenly sours with the presence of a negative figure. In the Church's attempt to demonize wise women, this antagonist is commonly a witch. Yet it is only because of the challenges presented by the Shadow figure that the hero achieves transformation and a happy ending. The Shadow archetype is that part of ourselves to which we deny existence. It is the mirror into which we are afraid to look.

In "Beauty and the Beast," the virginal Beauty is unbalanced in her love for her father. The sexual element of love is missing, as is appropriate in this dynamic. But Beauty unleashes the passionate Shadow after asking her father to bring her a white rose from his travels. Unselfish and virtuous, this is a very different request from the extravagant gifts her sisters demand. It is Beauty's innocence that unleashes a terrible situation for her father when he unthinkingly plucks the flower from the Beast's garden and is punished for this act. By keeping his youngest daughter a child, so in love with him that she would deny herself sexual awakening, the father is preventing Beauty from entering womanhood and fulfilling her destiny to become a complete human being. Enter the Beast, who accepts Beauty's offer to live with him in exchange for her father's freedom—and immediately falls in love with her. He repeatedly asks Beauty to marry him, but she refuses to do so. After a period of to-ing and fro-ing between her father's house and the Beast's castle (signifying Beauty's conflicting feelings for these male figures), Beauty realizes that the Beast needs her more and, should she not return to him, will die. She promises to be the Beast's wife if he stays alive, becoming aware that she has fallen in love with him. The Beast's physical ugliness represents the virginal belief that sexual love is menacing or repulsive. At her total acceptance of him, the Beast transforms into a handsome young prince and the two live happily ever after. This is a sweet story on a superficial level, but unraveled it is highly symbolic of the need to embrace our sexual natures and make the passage from innocent youth to sexually active adults. This theme of sexual awakening is also key to the story of Persephone (see p. 56).

Be aware that the dysfunctional archetypal patterns you explore as you work through this book have probably served you well in the past; therefore, be grateful to them for guiding you thus far. You also have the choice of embracing ones that better empower you for the pit stop of life in which you now find yourself. The purpose of this book is to help you make informed choices.

creating an altar

When undergoing any kind of self-development work, it is helpful to have a focal point to help motivate you and remind you of your new vision for your life. While journal work (see pp. 38–39) is invaluable in this process, unless you develop a daily ritual of putting down your thoughts on paper; you are likely to be fired up and enthusiastic for a few days or weeks after reading this book and then begin to lose momentum.

Creating an altar on which you can keep your journal, and other items of significance, will help to focus your attention on the spiritual journey you are about to undertake. Therefore, this place needs to be somewhere prominent, preferably on a window ledge or piece of furniture that you see last thing at night and first thing in the morning. A bedside table is ideal.

Your Goddess altar is the sacred space on which you will place any object that you feel reminds you of the Goddess theme and qualities you wish to integrate into your life. It should be a dynamic cornucopia of colors, shapes, and artifacts you associate with your chosen Goddess(es).

This is your unique, sacred space and therefore it is the personal significance that your altar items hold for you that is important. Trust your intuition. As you read through each of the Goddess examples and decide which one(s) are relevant to you, put it out to the Universe to bring your attention to objects that will enhance and beautify your altar and make it meaningful. Get into the habit of attending to your altar every day, making changes as you see fit.

Suggestions for your altar

* Goddess images
* Goddess symbols (see individual Goddess pages)
* Colored and/or scented candles
* Crystals
* Items of clothing
* Flowers
* Textured paper
* Statues
* Jewelry
* Incense sticks
* Books (including your journal)
* Fragrance

An Athena altar

Here is a list of items that I have collected and keep on my Athena (see pp. 64–65) altar:

* My journal
* Affirmation cards
* A piece of iron, signifying strength
* A toy snake, one of the symbols of Athena
* A small silver shield
* An image of an unidentified Goddess whom I consider to be Athena
* A pottery owl, symbol of Athena's wisdom
* A picture of Athens, taken when I was on vacation
* A photograph of me wearing a turquoise dress at a Goddess-invoking ceremony in which I chose to personify Athena
* A single terminated (pointed) chunk of purple fluorite, associated with discernment, rationality, and intuition – all Athena traits.

keeping a journal

Go into any stationery or art shop and you will find a range of beautifully bound journals in which to chronicle the awakening of your Goddess energy. Choose one that appeals to you, not just visually, but with regard to how it feels, the quality and texture of the paper, and its size, depending on whether or not you want it to be portable. I love starting a new journal, identifying those creamy blank pages with a fresh start and fertile beginnings. I experience a sense of expectancy as I finger each page. You may wish to buy a new pen – perhaps one that can be filled with brightly colored ink – so that the whole experience is given greater meaning and purpose than other forms of writing that you may engage in, thus separating your journal writing from other kinds.

Get into the habit of writing down the insights you gain from working through this book, preferably daily, perhaps just before you settle for the night. Light a scented candle and put on soothing music or Nature sounds if this helps you relax and be more creative. Enjoy the experience of recording the inner journey as you awaken the Goddess within you.

Why keep a journal?

There are many good things about keeping a journal, which is a record of your inner life in the same way that a diary is usually a record of outer experiences:

* It is a comforting ritual and provides invaluable psycho-spiritual security
* You have a record of important insights that come to you during moments of introspection or silence that might otherwise be forgotten or lost
* Like a diary, you are able to chart your progress and have the option of reviewing past challenges to see how your attitudes and behavior have changed
* It provides tangible proof of the value of personal development work, helping you stay motivated and focused on your goals.

Who do you think you are?

Open your journal to a blank page and head it: "I think I am...." Use these questions:

1. How do you feel about being a woman? List twenty words you associate with femaleness.

2. Have you ever thought you would prefer to be a man? In what circumstances do these thoughts arise?

3. What do you like about yourself? List fifty positive traits.

4. What aspects of your character do you consider "negative?"

5. What positive spin can you find for each negative trait?

6. What messages did you receive in childhood about the relationship between males and females? What was the dynamic between your parents? How did it inform your beliefs? Were you treated differently than opposite-sex siblings? What attitudes underpinned your parents' behavior?

7. What kinds of women do you get on with best? Which do you dislike? Why? What does this say about you?

8. Which magazines and newspapers do you read? What messages do they promote about womens' role in society? How do you feel about these messages? Do they align with your own beliefs? How do they affect how you feel about being a woman?

9. If you wrote a book that reflects your life what title would you give it? Is your heroine young and innocent, tentatively making her way through life, facing its dangers? Does your story revolve around a key relationship? Do you resonate with the story of a self-sufficient woman, wise in the ways of the world?

10. Looking at the chart of Goddesses (pp. 130–131), which appeal to you? What associated words align most with your life? Explore each word in your journal. Which are aspects that you have and don't want? Why? Which attributes or themes are missing from your life?

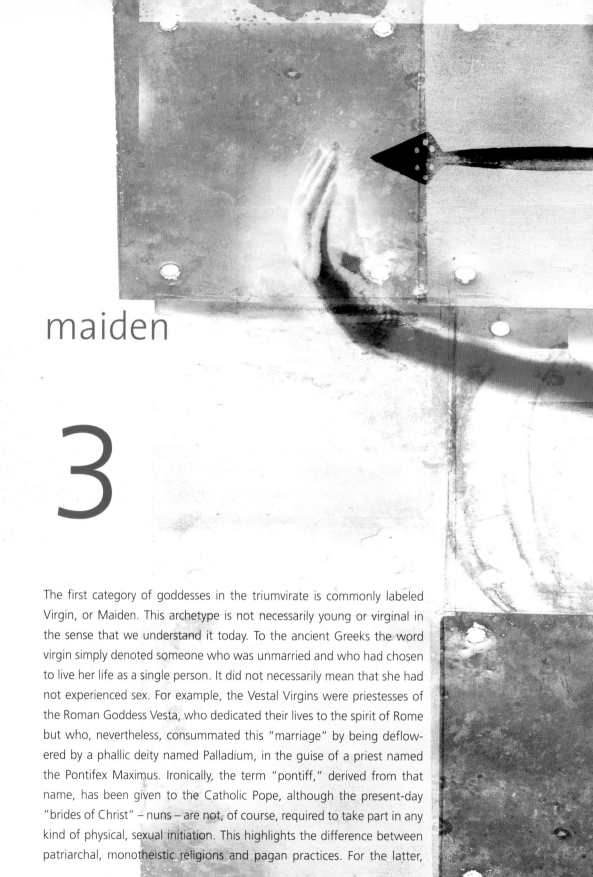

maiden

3

The first category of goddesses in the triumvirate is commonly labeled Virgin, or Maiden. This archetype is not necessarily young or virginal in the sense that we understand it today. To the ancient Greeks the word virgin simply denoted someone who was unmarried and who had chosen to live her life as a single person. It did not necessarily mean that she had not experienced sex. For example, the Vestal Virgins were priestesses of the Roman Goddess Vesta, who dedicated their lives to the spirit of Rome but who, nevertheless, consummated this "marriage" by being deflowered by a phallic deity named Palladium, in the guise of a priest named the Pontifex Maximus. Ironically, the term "pontiff," derived from that name, has been given to the Catholic Pope, although the present-day "brides of Christ" – nuns – are not, of course, required to take part in any kind of physical, sexual initiation. This highlights the difference between patriarchal, monotheistic religions and pagan practices. For the latter,

sexual expression was something to be celebrated and revered. Female sexuality is a powerful creative force that can be positively unleashed if we stop subscribing to the belief that it is wicked or dirty.

The term virgin – even in its ancient sense – is not wholly true of all the goddesses featured in this section. The word implies lack of contamination, as we might use it when talking about virgin soil, meaning soil unpolluted by pesticides or any other physical or chemical interference. As an analogy, we call the first pressing of olives, in which the oil is extracted without the application of heat, "virgin" olive oil – "heat" often synonymous with passion or emotion. Athena and Artemis were certainly passionate, although not about men. And Persephone, at least in the later rendition of this myth, was contaminated when she was raped by Hades. The psyches of all five of the goddesses mentioned in this chapter have been penetrated by men in ways other than the physical, hence the word Maiden is used to describe these mythological characters. However, this does not imply that this archetype is only evident in early life. One of the dysfunctional aspects of this archetype is the child-woman teetering dangerously on the border between childlike innocence and adult sexual expression.

The three main Maiden goddesses outlined in the following pages have positive characteristics in common, with which you might identify, either as a trait you currently possess or one that you wish to cultivate. This is particularly so when we look at the early, nonviolent, matriarchal version of the Persephone myth. All these goddesses demonstrate a clear focus on living their lives as they choose. They exemplify the freedom to live in their own nontraditional way, unencumbered by patriarchal standards, and demonstrate a tendency to dedicate themselves to a cause that is important to them. Each one achieves this in a different way.

Artemis chooses to separate herself completely from the world of men, preferring to create a domain for herself with her sisterhood of nymphs in the wilds of Nature. She is the archetypal feminist, an independent female spirit who is totally self-reliant. Artemis pursues her interests without male approval. Her identity and self-worth are based on who she is and what she accomplishes for herself rather than that of the man she is associated with or married to. She may be found in the laboratory, working late into the night on a scientific project. Or she may be working behind the scenes to bring about social reform or in support of a cause she is passionate about. There are many Artemis women in history to whom we should be grateful for their utter dedication to their life mission, which sometimes has required them to remain single and even celibate. Two famous examples are Florence Nightingale and Queen Elizabeth I of England, both of whom eschewed partnership to dedicate themselves to their destinies.

Kwan Yin's defiance of her father and the strength with which she pursued a vision running counter to that expected in male-dominated China seems at odds with her gentle, empathetic nature. But, when we have learned to embrace the paradoxes of life it is much easier to accept such inconsistencies of Nature. Rather than accede to her father's wish for her to marry into wealth, Kwan Yin – a Bodhisattva rather than a goddess – devoted herself to prayer. The strength and wisdom she embodied helped her to face both her father and the ruler of the dead who kept souls in bondage, unable to be reincarnated. Today, Kwan Yin is worshipped right across China and in Chinese communities all over the world as Mother of Mercy, Compassion, and Healing. She is revered for her dedication to suffering souls seeking inner peace. In contemporary life, Kwan Yin is personified by those women who dare to stand up against a dictatorial regime and stick to what they believe in, even if it costs them their lives. She is the ultimate goddess of values; she knew what was important to her in life, and her attitude and behavior was completely in alignment with that.

Persephone has a similar cause to Kwan Yin – that of looking after the souls in the Underworld. But according to the patriarchal version of the story (see p. 56) she had to undergo dramatic psychological changes before embracing her mission. This involved her abduction and rape by the God of the Underworld, Hades. Persephone's rite of passage from childhood into maidenhood transforms her into queen of that realm. In their male arrogance, the modifiers of the original story suggest that it is through sexual initiation that a female matures into a powerful woman. However it happens, whatever the trigger may be to cause this rebirth, the Persephone archetype accepts her life mission, turning even the most undesirable circumstances into a personal victory. This story also highlights the importance of compromise between various relationships, in this case between the needs of Persephone, her husband, Hades, and her mother, Demeter, as well as balancing the various facets of personal life purpose.

A key theme linking all of these Maiden Goddesses – with the exception of Blodeuwedd – is their roles as daughters. With Athena and Kwan Yin it is their relationship with their fathers that is key, while for Artemis and Persephone it is that with their mothers. Thus there is an interdependent association with this archetype in which it is clear that, while you are the product of your culture, upbringing, and life experiences, you also have free will. The Maiden mythologies highlighted here reveal that you always have the choice to be who you want to be: you can react positively or negatively to life's challenges.

As has been stated many times by spiritual teachers and others, it is not what happens to you that shapes your life, but your attitude about what happens to you. This is illustrated in the story of Persephone, who eventually chooses to come to terms with her fate, gaining greater maturity and self-ownership from her experience than she might have otherwise. I believe the greatest cause of personal suffering is the internal struggle between what we think we want and what we are meant to have. Persephone's destiny was to become Queen of the Underworld, a fearful and potentially hateful place, but a place where in which she could create an existence of personal value. After an initial period of resistance, Persephone surrendered to her fate and her success enhanced not only her life but her whole environment. A present-day example

of this is described in *Man's Search for Meaning*, written by psychiatrist and World War II concentration camp survivor, Viktor E. Frankl. He was incarcerated in Nazi death camps and endured years of unspeakable horror, but observed that there were always choices to be made. No one can take away that ultimate human freedom – to choose your attitude. Prisoners who looked for and found meaning, even in such a situation, could transcend their circumstances and survive, sanity and dignity intact.

Life expects something from each of us. It is our uniqueness that makes our existence so important. The Maiden archetypes offer inspiring examples of what you can do once you have chosen to accept that responsibility and live your life according to your innermost values, talents, and purpose.

Lunar themes Each of the three major Goddess archetypes – Maiden, Mother, and Wise Woman – is associated with the Moon. The same Indo-European root, from which the word "moon" is derived, is associated with other words, including menstruation, mentor, and mentality. Early pagan calendars were based on the female menstrual cycle, since this correlated with the phases of the Moon. Evidence of this custom has been found among ancient Chinese and Mayan artifacts. The Gaels used the same word for both menstruation and calendar, and the Roman word for the measurement of time – mensuration – literally means "knowledge of menses." Time was one of the concepts created by the Great Mother Goddess across many early cultures. One legend states that the Moon is the repository for earthly treasures that have been wasted, including time and unfulfilled intentions.

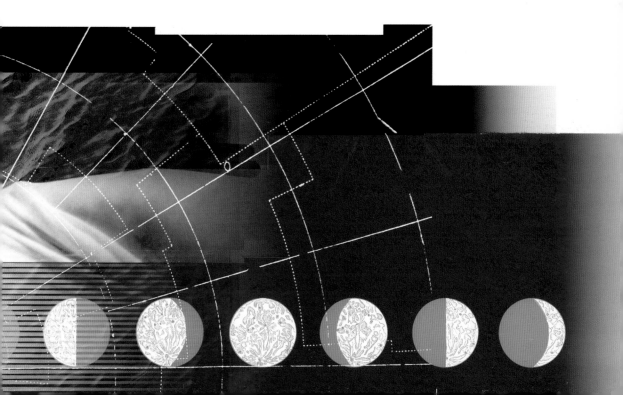

artemis
the goddess of hunting, woodlands, and fertility

Queen and huntress, chaste and fair
Now the sun is laid to sleep
Seated in thy silver chair
State in wonted manner keep
Ben Jonson, *Hymn to Diana*

When Zeus' wife, Hera (see pp. 84–89), discovered Leto's pregnancy by her philandering husband, she sent the serpent Python to torment the beautiful Nature deity. Hera also put a curse on Leto, preventing her from giving birth anyplace where the Sun shone. Eventually, Leto escaped to the island of Ortygia, where she gave birth to Artemis. Delivering her twin brother, Apollo, the young Artemis – only days old – acted as comforter and midwife to her mother. When she was introduced to her father, the young Artemis so entranced him that Zeus promised to give her anything she wanted. Artemis asked for all the things with which she has traditionally been associated: a silver bow, a full quiver of arrows, a pack of hunting hounds, a sisterhood of nymphs, the freedom to roam the mountains and wilderness – and eternal chastity.

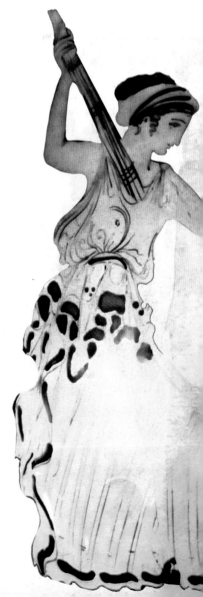

Tales abound of Artemis' fierce loyalty toward loved ones, as well as her mercilessness against anyone hurting or abusing them. For example, when Niobe, an Anatolian mountain goddess, foolishly boasted that she had many children, while Leto had only two, the proud mother asked her daughter Artemis to effect retribution. The huntress killed all of Niobe's offspring, causing their grief-stricken parent to be turned into a block of stone, from which a trickling fountain thereafter constantly "wept."

Artemis illuminates the paradox of the Goddess as life giver (in her role as patron of childbirth) and harbinger of death. She typifies the natural empathetic gift women have with their environment and the things that dwell in it. One of the key characteristics of a successful hunter is respect for their prey, by which they ensure their ongoing safety. In addition, hunters must be able intuitively to understand the nature of those whom they seek to kill, in order to be able to track them and anticipate their next moves.

olympian lineage

Artemis was the offspring of Zeus' extramarital liaison with Leto, a Nature deity and twin sister of Sun deity Apollo, the God of poetry, prophecy, the healing arts, and music. Said to be the oldest and most popular of the Greek Goddesses, the cult of Artemis – known to the Romans as Diana – was worshipped at the famous temple at Ephesus. Here was built a many-breasted statue of the Goddess, illustrating her position as nurturer of all humanity, in the same way that the wildlife with which she is associated suckles its young.

Symbols
* Silver bow and arrow
* She-Bear (protector of the young)
* The Lioness (regal qualities and hunting prowess)
* Moon
* Wildlife (elusiveness and sensitivity)

Theme   Self-ownership
Key role   The independent adventurer
Life lesson To ensure that your strong emotional boundaries do not become prison walls

Other Artemis roles
* Sister
* Feminist
* Competitor
* Parent (especially to mother)
* Wild woman
* Predator
* Avenger

Qualities

Functional	Dysfunctional
Independent	Uncompromising
Adventurous	Overly competitive
Self-reliant	Vengeful
Nurturing	Merciless
Passionate	Superior
Free-spirited	Invulnerable
Protective (of others)	Armored (of self)

present-day artemis

If you have ever felt alienated by urban living, have wanted to escape civilization to live quietly and alone, surrounded only by Nature and beloved pets, or have been drawn to occupations that involve solitary outdoor work – particularly involving conservation and animals – then you will have experienced Artemis in your life. She is the driving force behind women who are attracted to traditionally male careers, such as car mechanics, engineering, forestry, or truck driving, or who dedicate their lives to achieving in a sport.

Artemis exhibits the same independence and spirit as Athena, but her focus is on different things. For Artemis, it is not her intellect that is her driving force, but her drive for physical freedom. Regardless of age, Artemis is the stereotypical tomboy, the woman who loves the rugged lifestyle her more sophisticated sisters could not stomach. Athletic and with abundant physical energy, she is frequently labeled "one of the boys," and as such finds herself isolated from both men and women who do not understand, and thus, fear her. There is often a sense of psychological isolation from humanity, which the Artemis archetype highlights by withdrawing from the world.

When you come under the influence of Artemis you might begin to question your sexual orientation. Many Artemis women experiment with lesbianism, although this is by no means always the case. When this happens, an Artemis may become drawn into a sexual relationship that is incidental to her desire to develop a deep companionship with another woman whom she recognizes as sharing the same values and goals. Motherhood is not a strong focus for the Artemis woman. She likes children, but may have no desire for offspring. Even when she finds herself with a family, the desire for solitary pursuits and the strong draw of the outdoors may mean that her children have to learn at a very early age to become as self-sufficient as their mother.

In her fully functional form, Artemis is the perfect example of a woman who owns herself, who is whole and complete without a man. However, as you will discover through the following self-exploratory questions and affirmations, there may be a deep-seated wound that needs to be healed. One of these involves the reasons why an Artemis woman may find herself shying away from intimacy with others. If an Artemis child was chided by her parents or made to feel unfeminine for preferring dirt to dolls or animals to academia, she may have withdrawn from society in order to protect herself against future psychological abuse. While independence is a characteristic to be applauded, removing oneself from society denies the joy of true intimacy with other human beings. It also denies society the value of seeing a wonderfully centerd, self-reliant woman in action.

The Artemis archetype, as illustrated by stories of the goddess' acts of vengeance against foolish but not necessarily bad individuals, tends to see life in terms of black and white, such as the claim: If you are not for me, you must be against me. Artemis's strong competitive drive can be extremely alienating and she can exhibit a superiority complex that prevents the formation of friendships. All of this emphasizes the need to ensure that when the Artemis drive is strong, you do not imprison yourself within your strong emotional boundaries.

How to develop Artemis

* Set aside some quiet, undisturbed time.
* Sit comfortably before your altar and relax. Let the objects inspire you.
* Light a scented candle or some incense to create a contemplative atmosphere.
* Center yourself until you reach a state of calm receptivity, breathing deeply and regularly.
* Focus on the questions or issues you wish to explore. Let your inner wisdom and creativity get to work.
* Afterward, record your discoveries and insights in your journal.

Self-exploratory questions

1. True intimacy requires a level of comfort with vulnerability. What do "intimacy" and "vulnerability" mean to you? To what extent have you developed truly intimate relationships in your life?

2. How is the "wilderness woman" within you expressed? In what ways are you giving your inherent spirit of adventure and desire for exploration a completely free rein?

3. Think of occasions when you may have judged others overly harshly. How often do you find yourself shackled by "black and white" thinking? What might you do to change this?

4. How might your self-protective nature be preventing you from forming deeper friendships?

5. To what extent is the help you give to others practical rather than emotional?

6. Is your desire to be alone based on an inner strength or a reaction to a sense of being an "outsider"? How might you align your need for solitude with fully participating in society?

7. What kind of relationships have you had with men in the past? Have they been principally competitive, brotherly, friendly, and companionable rather than sexual? How do you really feel about that?

8. Do you place relationships secondary to your work or principal life interest (e.g., a sport or hobby)? Is that hierarchy currently appropriate for you? If not, how might you effect a change?

9. What do you associate with the term "grown-up"? Would you describe yourself in that way? What, if anything, do you fear about adulthood?

10. How balanced is your life? Do you express yourself equally in the areas of work, relationships (including lovers and family), social life, personal development, hobbies, community projects, health, and spirituality?

Affirmations

∗ I am learning to be comfortable with vulnerability; I accept that it is a sign of strength, not weakness.

∗ Self-reliance does not mean isolation – I am proud to demonstrate my independence within society.

∗ I commit to demonstrating compassion before judging others harshly.

∗ I choose to express my adventurous nature in many creative ways.

∗ In order to experience deeper relationships, I need to demonstrate compassion and empathy.

∗ I am a strong, balanced, independent woman with clear emotional boundaries, and yet I encourage intimacy with others.

kwan yin
goddess of serenity, good fortune, and peaceful
enlightenment

In the lands of the universe there is no place
Where She does not manifest Herself...
Compassion wondrous as a great cloud
Pouring spiritual rain like nectar
Quenching the flames of distress!
The Lotus Sutra

As the only child of a wealthy but cruel man, Miao Shan (Kwan Yin's earthly name) was to be married to someone who would confer riches and status on the family. However, the girl had always desired to become a nun. Although her father knew of her childhood passion to serve others, he chose to disregard his daughter's wishes and went ahead with the wedding preparations, foolishly believing that Miao Shan's silence and disinterest on the matter meant that he would soon have this challenging daughter off his hands. Miao Shan prayed for hours, bewildering her father, who decided to punish her for her intransigence by locking her in a tower, with only dry rice to eat and no company. Still, Miao Shan prayed and meditated, refusing to be fitted for her wedding dress. Furious with her defiance, Miao Shan's father ordered his soldiers to kill her. The kind and gentle girl had always been loved by everyone, but fearing the wrath of their master, the men lead Miao Shan to a forest, where they executed her. As she was about to enter Heaven, she heard a soul on Earth crying out. She then turned back toward life on Earth and committed to living in this world until everyone who is suffering is free from misery and pain. Because of this compassionate, selfless act, the girl was transmuted in Kwan Yin. She sits on the island of P'u T'o Shan, answering all those who pray to her.

To this day Kwan Yin is widely worshipped in China and Chinese communities. Eastern households generally have at least one statue of her in the home – a being draped in a white veil. At the temple of Miao Feng Shan, near Peking, devotees make an annual pilgrimage, asking Kwan Yin to heal them of illnesses and rid them of life's miseries and difficulties.

chinese pantheon

The ancient Chinese arranged their deities as mirrors of their earthly administrations, with strictly hierarchical rankings, at times as no more than supernatural civil servants in the way they constantly reported to their sovereign Lord Jade. One of the key differences between the Chinese pantheon and that of other cultures is that the function of the gods persist, while the deities can be replaced by new ones, the Chinese regarding their gods as men deified after death, not divinities. The male-focused structure of ancient Chinese society is evident in the way that the principal divinities representing the Sun, rain, thunder, and wind as well as long life and happiness are all male. The Moon has a female personage – Ch'ang-o.

Symbols
* Lotus blossom – emblem of purity, beauty, and spirituality
* Vase – storing "sweet dew" or waters of compassion
* Various gemstones – on which wishes are granted

Theme	Fearless adherence to core values, living your values, integrity
Key role	Caregiver
Life lesson	To be in service to others while caring fully for oneself

Qualities

Functional	Dysfunctional
Altruistic	Self-sacrificing
Compassionate	Unrealistic
Unconditional love	Rescuing – codependent
Fearless	Lack of life balance
Holding clear values	Neglect of Self
Integrity	None
In service to others	None

Other Kwan Yin roles
* Bodhisattva – an individual on the threshold of enlightenment
* Great Mother of China
* Healer of the Sick
* Lady who cares for mother and children in distress

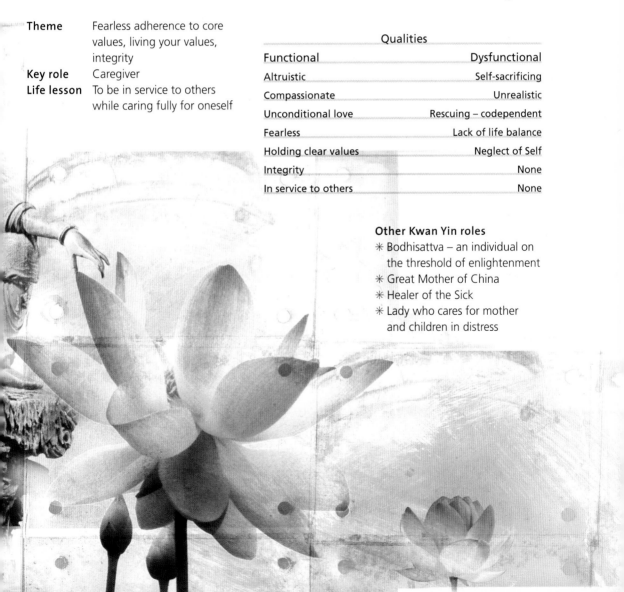

present-day kwan yin

Few of us would claim to be as single-minded, brave, and compassionate as Kwan Yin. Nevertheless, there often beats within us the hint of a mission or passion that we are afraid to acknowledge, let alone pursue. Women embodying the Kwan Yin archetype may have known from an early age what their purpose is in life. This tends to involve one of the caring professions, such as becoming a doctor, nurse, or teacher, or following a religious or spiritual vocation. Like this oriental goddess, this requires single-minded determination in the face of opposition, possibly lack of acceptance of this vision on the part of a parent or partner.

When the Kwan Yin archetype is a strong driving force in a woman's life, she overcomes all odds and steadfastly lives with integrity, according to her own values. However, the desire to care for others needs to be balanced with self-care, ensuring that your health, well-being, needs, and desires are as important as those for whom you might sacrifice everything.

How to develop Kwan Yin

* Set aside some quiet, undisturbed time.
* Sit comfortably before your altar and relax. Let the objects inspire you.
* Light a scented candle or some incense to create a contemplative atmosphere.
* Center down until you reach a state of calm receptivity, breathing deeply and regularly.
* Focus on the questions or issues you wish to explore. Let your inner wisdom and creativity get to work.
* Afterward, record your discoveries and insights in your journal.

Self-exploratory questions

1. What career aspirations did you have as a child that may not have been developed in adulthood? Is there a part of you that wishes to take a different life path to the one you are currently on? What is stopping you?
2. How do you handle opposition to your deepest desires?
3. Who in your life has actively remonstrated against something you passionately believe in? What happened?
4. Spiritual teachers through the centuries have pointed out that the greater your pain and suffering, the greater your capacity to experience joy. How do you feel about this?
5. In your desire to serve and give to others, do you neglect your own needs? How might you achieve greater balance?
6. Why do you feel the need to care for others? Is this grounded in genuine unconditional love for humanity or are you subconsciously looking for ways in which to bolster your confidence, self-esteem, and desire for others to love and appreciate you?
7. When was the last time you prayed? How do you feel about your connection to the Divine?
8. To what extent do you experience a sense of destiny in your life? What might you do to strengthen this?

Simple chanting meditations

* Invoking the names of goddesses or saints has, through the ages, helped inspire altered states of consciousness. In China, it is believed that simply uttering Kwan Yin's name brings comfort to the sick and distressed.
* Whenever you wish to accelerate self-healing, either of a mental or physical kind, try chanting the name of Kwan Yin. Allow the repetition to clear your mind of all other concerns. Listen only to the sound of your voice, breathe deeply and evenly, and relax your body and mind. Be aware of sudden insights and calls to action that may come to you.
* Undertaking a walking meditation while chanting Kwan Yin's name is a powerful and extraordinarily fulfilling ritual.

persephone
mother's daughter, death goddess, queen of the underworld

He caught hold of her, protesting,
And he took her away, weeping, in his chariot of gold.
Homeric hymn

Hades, King of the Underworld, looking for a wife, approached Zeus, Persephone's father, to ask for her hand. However, Zeus knew that Persephone's protective mother, Demeter, would never agree and suggested kidnapping her. One day Persephone was entranced by a glorious narcissus. As she bent to pluck it, the Earth opened and Hades emerged. Scooping her up in his arms, they disappeared in moments. Demeter was grief-stricken and searched the Earth for nine days and nights, during which the world was threatened by famine as Demeter neglected to provide the harvest.

Meanwhile, Persephone, deeply affected by her violent kidnapping and rape, refused to eat. Hades, besotted with his bride, tried to tempt her to eat pomegranate seeds. He had been told by Zeus that the only way to bind Persephone to him would be to ensure that she ate while in his kingdom. However, Hades did not force his bride to eat and eventually she did so willingly. Alarmed by the hunger caused by Demeter's mourning, Zeus tried to reassure Demeter by telling her where her daughter was and dispatching Hermes to urge Hades to return the girl to her mother. Once reunited, Demeter asked if her daughter had eaten while in Hades. Persephone told her that Hades had forced her to do so, and Demeter feared that she had lost her daughter forever. However, a compromise was struck. It was agreed that Persephone would become Queen of the Underworld for four months of the year – in winter, when her mother went into mourning – and spend the rest of the year in the upper world with Demeter. Persephone did not readily accept her fate. Imprisoned in Hades, she became depressed, reflecting her struggle with the loss of childhood and fear of maturity. But Persephone realized that she could either continue her self-destructive behavior or embrace the Shadow and find fulfilment. She chose the latter and became Queen of the Underworld.

olympian lineage

The daughter of Zeus and Corn Goddess, Demeter (see pp. 78–83), little is known of the conception of Persephone in Greek mythology. However, her story, and that of her mother, Demeter, is central to the Eleusinian mysteries, whose religion and secret ceremonies held sway among agrarian races in ancient Greece prior to the arrival of Christianity.

Symbols
* Narcissus, symbol of spring, rebirth, sexual awakening
* Pomegranate, ancient symbol of uterine fertility
* Two faces, highlighting link between mother and daughter
* The Underworld, signifying the unconscious or shadow side of our natures

Theme — Sexual maturity; a transformational journey or rite of passage from innocent maiden to powerful woman

Key role — Discovery of sexual self

Life lesson — Change does not mean death, but transformation

Qualities	
Functional	**Dysfunctional**
Surrendering	Dependent
Adventurous	Fear of change
Balanced	Depressive/despairing
Empowered through adversity	Fails to see positive
Recognition of personal power	Passive

Other Persephone roles
* Kore ("young girl" or "daughter")
* The Roman goddess, Proserpina
* Grain Maiden

present-day persephone

The fear of moving away from childhood and into womanhood, involving the pain of menstruation and childbirth, is one that does not just affect young girls. Many of us can hold our hands up to certain behavior (see right), all of which demonstrates clinging to attitudes inappropriate for the powerful women we really are.

In an age when every day can present a challenge and when there seems no end to the chaos and extreme busy-ness of our lives, it is tempting to revert to being a child. After all, that was the time when we were not expected to take on responsibilities, when life (at least for the lucky majority) was filled with play and fun, and sex was viewed as something distasteful, designed only for grown-ups. So many fanciful and erroneous stories about sex and puberty are spread among young children that it is not surprising that adulthood is something which many of us decide to avoid for as long as possible. Childish misconceptions about sex, perhaps fuelled by inadequate education, can make us squeamish and can contribute to girls refusing to "grow up" and become the mature, powerful women they really are.

Persephone women are extremely passive. They rely on others to influence their lives because they are so comfortable with the status quo. There is always safety in remaining where we are –

Persephone behavior

* Allowing our mothers to emotionally blackmail us into agreeing to do something we do not wish to do
* Acting as if we are unintelligent, impractical females in order to make the men in our lives feel better about themselves and more in charge
* Deliberately holding back from developing our careers or lives, generally because we do not think we would be able to cope with, or even deserve, the success and will not take the risk of failing
* Calling our parents "Mommy" and "Daddy" even after we have become parents ourselves
* Pretending that we are helpless Maidens in order to seem more attractive to men

physically, psychologically, emotionally, and spiritually. In those places they feel safe, unthreatened by the enormous change and chaos that seems to affect everyone else so detrimentally.

However, change is inevitable. Just as spring must eventually give way to summer and summer to autumn, then autumn to winter, our lives conform to a never-ending cyclical growth and development that cannot be prevented. After all, to stand still is to stagnate, just as water that does not flow becomes foul, preventing anything from surviving in it for long. Rather than rely on others for our identity, life requires us to find and embrace our mission, regardless of the circumstances. This is the challenge – to become the best people we possibly can, and to fulfil ourselves, even though the circumstances in which we find ourselves may seem less than ideal at the time.

The extreme violence of Persephone's abduction and rape by Hades and her expansion and transformation from passive, sub-missive child to powerful Queen of the Underworld, reminds us that only when faced with a real challenge do we get the opportunity to show what we are really made of.

Persephone women need to discover the central meaning to their lives and find out what they are truly put on this Earth to achieve. They need to find their own mission in life. Only through that can they stop looking back over their shoulders to an earlier, seemingly more carefree, life, and grasp the opportunities to carve their own destinies and become equal to those who once had power over them.

How to develop Persephone
* Set aside some quiet, undisturbed time.
* Sit comfortably before your altar and relax. Let the objects inspire you.
* Light a scented candle or some incense to create a contemplative atmosphere.
* Center down until you reach a state of calm receptivity, breathing deeply and regularly.
* Focus on the questions or issues you wish to explore. Let your inner wisdom and creativity get to work.
* Afterward, record your discoveries and insights in your journal.

Self-exploratory questions

1. In what ways have you become gripped by passivity? Even when circumstances seem less than ideal, how can you turn poison into medicine and discover true purpose and meaning in your life?

2. How can you better balance receptiveness and surrender with energy and focus?

3. Where might you be holding yourself back in order to avoid responsibilities that may seem overwhelming? In your career? By putting off having a child? By avoiding becoming involved with someone? In setting more appropriate boundaries between yourself and your mother?

4. Does life seem to just happen to you, or do you take charge of your own destiny? Examine where this has been a good thing, and where it has not.

5. How much do you blame other people for "ruining" your life? Think of three or four situations – your mother did not want you to leave home for college, your husband failed to support you in your career, or your boss never recognized your potential. Ask yourself if it was appropriate for you to give away your power to another person. To what extent are you prepared to take responsibility for the way your life has turned out?

6. What kind of relationship do you, or did you, have with your mother? To what extent do you enjoy a mutually respectful interdependence?

7. What do you fear or dislike most about being a "grown-up"? What is the source of that negative emotion and what can you do to transcend it?

8. Have you ever celebrated your emergence into womanhood with a ritual? What kind of images and rites might you include in such a ceremony? What do these reveal about how you feel about becoming a woman?

9. Who in your life has become your surrogate mother? Is this relationship based on equality?

10. How do you feel about the word "commitment"? What decisions are you currently putting off, either because you do not want to accept responsibility for your choice or because you fear cutting yourself off from other possibilities?

An exercise in commitment

Because Persephone archetypes prefer to play at life rather than become adults and accept responsibility for their choices, they frequently procrastinate – about their career, promotion, partner, or whether or when to have children. If you recognize this tendency, try this exercise:

* Imagine that you are viewing your life objectively. Take a "third-party" stance on one current area of indecision – personal or professional.
* Write down a sentence about this challenge on a blank sheet of paper, such as "I don't know whether I really want a more challenging role in this organization."
* Draw a line down the center of the sheet and head the two columns: "Yes" and "No" points. Now brainstorm reasons for and against.
* Revisit this list over a week, adding more pros and cons.

At the end of this time see which column contains the most points. During this process be aware of what your heart, as well as your head, is telling you about the best choice to make.

* If the "Yes" column has the longest list, take this as a sign for action. If the "No" column has more entries, reexamine each of the points and ask whether there are any fears, outmoded attitudes, or behavior underpinning them.

blodeuwedd
the orphan archetype

This Welsh Maiden Goddess, like Athena, is connected with the owl, but for a very different reason. She was created out of flowers (her name means "flowerface") by two wizards, as a wife for a young god named Lleu Llaw Gyffes, who had been cursed by his mother, Aranrhod, with never being able to take a wife belonging to any existing race. Although exceptionally beautiful, Blodeuwedd's personality was, in turn, charming and treacherous. She fell in love with a forest hunting god, Gronw Pebyr, and together they plotted the death of Lleu. This was no easy task, since her husband's demise depended on being killed very specifically – from a spear in the side, which was to enter the body at a particular angle. As punishment for this crime, Blodeuwedd was turned by one of the wizards into an owl, a creature that comes out only at night and risks being molested by all other wild birds.

Present-day Blodeuwedd
* Believing you are nothing without a partner and that your sole purpose in life is to be somebody's wife
* Taking part in an inappropriate relationship and then, rather than being authentic about your feelings, choose faithlessness and perhaps even to destroy your partner in some way rather than admit your mistake
* Having a beautiful body, but lacking moral values and soul
* Realizing that beauty is demonstrated from within, without which there is no true humanity

Visual themes
* Owl – the bird she was condemned to live as after her treachery, because she could not be killed
* Meadowsweet, oak, and broom – Blodeuwedd was made of the blossoms, like a female Green Man
* Frankenstein's monster has strong links with this story of rejecting the role for which she was created, with tragic consequences

Dysfunctional qualities
Soulless

Child-woman

Unbalanced

The Blodeuwedd lesson
While it may appear, at face value, that Blodeuwedd has little to teach us (except in the art of treachery), she does highlight an important lesson. It is particularly pertinent to women who are physically very attractive, because there is a tendency for them to rely on their beauty. Psychological studies have demonstrated the extent to which physically appealing individuals tend to be paid more, get their wishes acceded to more readily, and generally find favor over and above those who are less alluring.

Going through life experiencing these kinds of instantly affirming reactions can, if one is not careful, affect the development of the personality and the spirit. Many of us have "glammed" ourselves up and fallen back on our sexuality as a means of persuading the opposite sex to do what we want. This kind of manipulative behavior is not helpful if it becomes our sole means of dealing with life's challenges.

Whenever we are tempted to do likewise, think of Blodeuwedd, the beautiful but soulless creature whose destructive nature caused so much pain, not least to herself. A well-developed, fully functioning human being has so many more inner resources at her disposal, including personality, intelligence, and charisma. Remember, Blodeuwedd's demise came about because she did not have the capacity for these in the first place. We do, and it is the responsibility of each of us to develop them.

athena
the warrior archetype

This Greek Warrior Goddess sprang, fully grown, from her father Zeus' head and was known as an accomplished strategist and mentor/supporter of heroic men, including Achilles and Ulysses. She represents many traits that some might consider "masculine," including choosing logic over intuition, intellect over emotion, and success over relationships. An extremely practical thinker, one of the symbols associated with Athena is the owl, representing this goddess's wisdom.

Present-day Athena
* Relating more to your father than your mother
* Preferring male to female company
* Having a tendency to live for your work
* Finding it difficult to become emotionally connected or intimate with others
* Living in your head at the expense of experiencing deep feelings
* Finding that others, particularly men, are intimidated by you
* Considering vulnerability to be a weakness

Symbols

* Female warrior
* Dramatic birth (springing from Zeus' head fully armed)
* Owl – symbol of wisdom
* Spider, or spinning wheel – connected with the story of Athena turning Arachne into a spider after she became angered by seeing a tapestry depicting Zeus' many infidelities
* Olive tree – Athena's gift to Athens, promoting olive cultivation
* Protection of soldiers during war, plus goldsmiths, potters, and weavers

Balancing your Athena archetype

1. Engage in at least one physical activity that connects you with your body, to offset the many intellectual pursuits you more naturally undertake.

2. Become actively involved in a female group, preferably one that has a non-work, charitable connection.

3. Get into the habit of listening meditatively to emotive music and explore your potential to become moved by it.

4. Consider the extent to which you wear protective "armor" – through certain attitudes or behavior when interacting with others, and look for ways in which you might develop enhanced emotional intelligence.

5. If possible, look for ways to reconnect with your mother, in order to help you develop your feminine side. Try not to act as if the two of you are from different planets.

6. Allow yourself to "feel" situations, rather than intellectually assess them. Consider what your heart is telling you rather than just your head.

7. Look to develop friendships with women, not just men. Remember that our lives become more balanced and enriched by those who are different from us and can offer a fresh perspective on life.

8. Learn to develop a love relationship with a partner for its own sake, rather than A) choosing someone because you think he has potential and can be groomed for success, or B) becoming an indispensable asset in a partnership, the power behind the throne.

Make sure that both of you focus on what you give to each other emotionally, rather than just becoming a "power couple."

mother

4

The second group of goddesses that we are about to explore is the Mother. That this archetype should be so universally worshipped is not surprising. Humans have long identified Earth as their mother, which is particularly apt since scientists now postulate that complex, organic molecules such as the body's RNA and DNA, may have developed from inorganic crystals of clay, so when we die we return to Gaia's womb. Some early cultures even buried their dead in the earth in the fetal position, suggesting a belief in returning the body to Mother Earth in order to facilitate a rebirth.

Viewed simply from the perspective of motherly love and devotion to their offspring, the following choices of Mother Goddess archetypes might not seem to fit the bill. And, on the face of it, they do not seem to have much in common. The stories about Isis and Osiris, Hera, and Zeus focus more on their marriages than the mothers' relation-

ships with their children. Isis and Demeter go to great lengths to support and protect their respective offspring, but Hera sent one of hers – the God of the Forge,
Hephaestus – out of Olympus because he had a disability. Plus, with each of these
archetypes, their relationships with other women are varied. Isis has a close bond
with her "shadow" in the guise of her sister, Nephthys, but neither Demeter nor
Hera is particularly known for their strong links with other females. Indeed,
Persephone's father is Zeus, the husband of Demeter's sister, Hera. In the latter's
case it was often the innocent victim of her husband's lust who was punished by the
jealous goddess, rather than her spouse.

The key purpose of the Mother archetype is to understand and
embrace the nature of change. If you accept that the purpose of life is to grow spiritually – to become enlightened in religious parlance or "self-actualized" as human-
istic psychologist, Abraham Maslow, describes it – then we must continually seek to
develop our full potential. However, as we all know, maintaining the status quo is
infinitely more comfortable. Therein lies a measure of control in an otherwise chaotic and uncertain world. Life will have none of that. The lesson of the Mother is that
if we do not face change willingly, then it will be forced upon us, in far more dramatic circumstances that we would otherwise choose. It is the concept of loss as a
catalyst for self-transformation that is the common link for the three major goddesses we are about to examine.

Separation and loss is a common theme in love stories; the "boy meets
girl, boy loses girl, boy finds girl again" story line is used as a basis for countless
films and plays. This, I believe, is the natural law related to the Mother archetype,
which continued to be acknowledged, even after the new patriarchal order, and its
values sought to subjugate and humiliate the Goddess (see Gaia, pp. 90–91).

Similar to the Maiden examples, each of the three major Mother
Goddesses in this chapter faces loss and achieves personal transformation in a very
different way. For Isis, this occurs with the death of her beloved husband, Osiris. This
Egyptian goddess is forced to dig deep into her inner resources (in this story the
marshes of the River Nile are a metaphor for venturing into the subconscious), in
order to transform not just herself but the reputation of her husband. Through her
efforts, Osiris is elevated from a lowly nature entity to a nationally worshipped god
and his immortality assured both through direct worship and the accession of his

son, Horus, to the throne of Egypt. It is no coincidence that Isis' sister, Nephthys, plays a pivotal role in this story. Nephthys is considered a clone, or shadow, of Isis, that part of her nature associated with the unconscious mind, intuition, and our deepest fears.

Demeter loses her daughter, Persephone, to sexual maturity and is plunged into deep depression because of the loss of her role as protector and nurturer. To the ancient Greeks this explained the onset of winter, when nothing seems to grow, and without adequate planning there is always the risk of famine and death. Demeter is the epitome of the good and generous mother, but in whose dysfunctional psyche lies the seeds of the smothering, destructive mother, who is so fixated on one role that she becomes inflexible and resistant to changing circumstances. Thwarted in her attempts to continue with her motherly role, Demeter risks destroying the whole of humanity. A fecund goddess, life relies on the mother to look beyond her immediate responsibility to her own children in order to fertilize her own existence and thus develop the contribution she can make to life generally.

As is demonstrated by Demeter's cyclical retreat into depression when Persephone goes back to spend some of the year with her husband, Hades, this lesson is a hard one for women to bear if this particular archetype is strongly formed in their personalities.

Hera's loss is just as painful and profound, revolving around her sense of personal identity and self-esteem. She becomes so bound up in the role of wife – as Demeter does in the role of mother – that she loses much of herself in the process. Her challenge is to rediscover that part of herself and become integrated sufficiently to be able to accept another person exactly as they are and thus love them unconditionally. It is said that Hera women have a tendency to change after marriage. It is not that they are different at all, just that they have taken off the mask of pretence and are showing their true colors. Hera might have ensured that her married life was more meaningful and satisfying if she had concerned herself less with Zeus' behavior and more with creating a fulfilling life for herself outside the role of wife.

This can be a very destructive archetype to deal with. As you will discover through Hera's story (see pp. 84–89), what is called for is the shedding of the part of "victim." Before we can trust others, we must have learned to trust ourselves. While there remain facets of ourselves that are unknown or unexplored, total self-belief and self-reliance are not possible. Thus, the Hera archetype projects her fears, often unfounded, onto a partner, whom she suspects of constantly betraying her with other women.

As soon as Hera let go of Zeus – hers being an emotional and psychological, as well as a geographical separation, then she learned that she could not only survive the loss but thrive as an accomplished woman in her own right. This is the Hera lesson: that each of us is whole of and by ourselves. We do not need a partner to validate or complete us.

Both Demeter and Isis reexplore the maternal instinct during their periods of separation from their loved ones. They share very similar experiences in taking on the role of nursemaid to other women's children – Isis at Byblos and Demeter at Eleusis. This articulates the need to risk developing other relationships. In both tales, the goddesses seek to make their charges immortal, but are prevented from doing so by the children's natural mothers, who, misunderstanding the nature of the ritual, fear for their offsprings' lives and scream out in horror, preventing the completion from taking place. This is the rational, human response to the offer of immortality. How many of us, given the choice and considering all that it would entail, would really want to live forever?

What each of the following three stories (Isis, Demeter, and Hera) demonstrates is the importance of rising above challenging circumstances, paradoxically by venturing deep inside oneself.

According to ancient belief, the archetypal Mother denoted what we now term "emotional intelligence" – the ability to nurture mutually supportive relationships with others. The most important lesson that we can learn from the Mother archetype is the value of "mothering" and supporting ourselves – physically, emotionally, and spiritually.

The inner journey
(after the Dalai Lama)

1. Finding great love and making great achievements always involve taking great risks in life. In other words, no gain without pain.

2. When you lose, do not lose the lesson; look for the purpose to your pain. Like the furnace that transforms base metals into gold, pain prepares us for the alchemical journey of resurrection.

3. Judge your success by what personal sacrifices you had to make – the valuable things that you had to give up – in order to get it.

isis

egyptian mother goddess of magic, devotion, and loyalty

I am Nature, the Universal Mother, mistress of all the
elements, primordial child of time, sovereign of all things
spiritual, queen of the dead, queen also of the immortal, the
single manifestation of all gods and goddesses that are. ...
Call me by my true name, namely, Queen Isis.
Apuleius, *The Golden Ass*, second century A.D.

Foolishly mistaking his sister for his wife, Isis, Osiris slept with
Nephthys, who conceived the jackal-headed Anubis. Driven by a
long-standing jealousy of his older brother, Seth (Nephthys' husband) plots the death of Osiris by preparing a sarcophagus made to
Osiris' measurements. Seth tricks his brother into lying in the sarcophagus, whereupon he secures the lid and throws it into the Nile,
drowning Osiris.

Distraught, Isis goes in search of her husband's body
and after a long journey through swamps (metaphor for the unconscious) finds Osiris, places the sarcophagus on the royal barge, and
plans to take him home for proper burial. During their travels, Isis
removes the lid of the coffin and lies with her dead husband,
becoming pregnant with their son, Horus. But before Isis can final-
ize the funeral arrangements, Seth finds Osiris' resting place and
cuts the body into fourteen pieces, which are then scattered to the
four winds. Isis has to face her loss once more and begins a new
journey, this time to collect the pieces of her husband's body. At
each location Isis fashions a replica limb or organ and gives it to a
priest to bury. Each one is compelled to swear that the whole of
Osiris' body rests in that grave. This clever ruse by Isis precludes Seth
from finding a single grave and desecrating it and ensures that her
husband achieves immortality throughout Egypt. The only piece of
Osiris that Isis cannot find is his penis, so she makes one out of gold
and, in some versions of the story, it is with this that she impreg-
nates herself. It is said that the image of the child Horus sitting on
the lap of his divine mother was borrowed by the Christians, who
renamed them the Madonna and Christ. Osiris only received divine
status after death, through the loyalty and devotion of Isis.

egyptian lineage

Daughter of Earth God, Geb, and Sky Goddess Nut, Isis is the twin sister of Osiris. The basic story of Isis and Osiris was recorded in the Pyramid Texts of the Old Kingdom, dating from c. 2649–2152 B.C.E., and in the Coffin Texts of the Middle Kingdom of c. 2040–1783 B.C.E. Supported by his wife Isis, Osiris is credited with the cultivation of wheat and barley throughout Egypt, thereby bestowing wealth and security on its people.

Isis, his sister-wife, was also originally a modest local deity, whose importance increased with his. With the establishment of the concept of divine kingship the Pharaohs proclaimed the gods to be their divine ancestors. They saw themselves as the living incarnations of Osiris and Isis' son, Horus.

Symbols
* Cat – a creature of independence and resourcefulness
* Throne – the hieroglyphic for Isis' name means "throne"
* Crown of cow horns – representing nourishing maternal power

Theme The permanence of human existence
Key role Redeemer
Life lesson Death must come before resurrection

Other Isis roles
* Primordial Great Goddess of Egypt
* Giver of Life
* Oldest of the Old
* Magician

Qualities	
Functional	Dysfunctional
Persistent	Martyr
Devoted	Cannot accept endings
Insightful	Self-sacrificing
Resourceful	Devious
Loyal	Mournful

present-day isis

Isis has two very important lessons to teach us in today's world. The first is the essential role that women can play as wives and mothers (though this is often considered old-fashioned today); the second is the great importance of the grieving process in the overall experience of healing.

Present-day society has tended to denigrate the importance of the wifely and the motherly role. This is because we place so little value on unpaid work, work that normally takes place in the home. Being a homemaker, looking after children, supporting one's spouse in all the little, practical ways that ease the stress of their jobs – all these things are considered, by many, to be less valuable than public and paid work.

By invoking the Isis archetype, we can rediscover our pride in the incomparable nurturing and life-giving force of the Mother Goddess. Isis' huge, protective wings have extensive reach, a metaphor for the way in which a mother's influence extends way beyond her immediate family unit. This is because it is only through

a loving, stable, supportive, and strong family bond that society is populated by empowered, confident, and productive individuals. When the Isis archetype is a strong presence in a woman she takes great pride in being her partner's loyal and devoted companion; someone who is equal and certainly complementary to her mate. After all, it is Isis' resourcefulness that elevates Osiris to a level of divinity and ensures that his heir then rules Egypt. This is very much a marriage based on mutual love and respect. Isis teaches us about the importance of flexibility through her many guises – as wife, consort, sister, divine mother, and magician. It is the latter role that alludes to the secret power of woman – the ability to give new life to that which once was dead.

Awakening Isis within you means that you acknowledge that before healing or resurrection can take place there must be a process of grieving to go through. In modern society we tend to want to rush through the various stages because we are so used to the "quick fix" and instant gratification. However, much is made in Egyptian accounts of the extended lamentations by Isis and her sister, Nephthys, over Osiris' death.

Now we examine the various facets of the grieving process and some positive "Isis action" points. For this exercise you will need to write in your journal.

How to develop Isis

* Set aside some quiet, undisturbed time.
* Sit comfortably before your altar and relax. Let the objects inspire you.
* Light a scented candle or some incense to create a contemplative atmosphere.
* Center down until you reach a state of calm receptivity, breathing deeply and regularly.
* Focus on the questions or issues you wish to explore. Let your inner wisdom and creativity get to work.
* Afterward, record your discoveries and insights in your journal.

The grieving process

Bear in mind that individuals experience these stages in different ways. Sometimes, like Isis' reexperience of loss, it is necessary to go back over a particular stage because that lesson needs to be reinforced. Some people move through stages quickly, others much more slowly. But whichever happens, trust that you will achieve your resurrection; like Isis' example, to effect true healing requires perseverance and a combination of introspection and action.

Modern psychologists tell us that there are five stages to the grieving process:
1. Shock   2. Denial   3. Depression   4. Anger   5. Acceptance

1. Shock It is important at this time of physical, mental, and emotional numbness to engage in the security of a ritual. Writing about how you feel in an unedited, non-judgmental way (even if it seems nonsensical) in your journal will offer a degree of psychological comfort and control at this chaotic and seemingly inexplicable time.

2. Denial This can be a lengthy and debilitating part of the grieving process, in which it is important not to downplay how much your loss really means to you or engage in "magical" thinking in which you convince yourself that your loss is only temporary and will be restored. Name your feelings as you write. Look at the fitness of things. If you have suddenly experienced redundancy or your partner has left you, honestly appraise the extent to which your values and those of your ex-partner were in true alignment.

3. Depression This much-misunderstood emotion is said to be unexpressed anger turned toward the Self. Jung referred to it as the "sticking point," whereby it is vitally important to get back in touch with your Higher Self, or spirit, to bring about essential healing. Write down the answers to question such as:
* Who are you?
* If you were to know, deep inside, why this loss has occurred, what would the reason be?
* What lesson is life trying to teach you through this experience?
* To whom or where should your unexpressed anger be more appropriately directed?

4. Anger We tend to be brought up to fear, and thus to avoid, this emotion, but it is an essential precursor to effecting change. Think of your anger as a positive force for good. Look for examples, both contemporary and historical, where a person's or a group's anger has caused great breakthroughs. Make a list of what you are grateful for in your life. What blessings continue to be heaped upon you, despite your loss? Every morning, focus on what is good about you and your life. It may help if you recall a similar experience in the past, in which you have had cause to grieve and truthfully acknowledge how you feel about it now, with hindsight.

5. Acceptance Now that you have completed the introspective work, it's time to take action, in order to bring your new life into being. This is not a stage of resignation but of surrender to your new role. Despite the burden placed upon Isis – both as a widow and single mother – she found within herself the power to do everything for herself, and the independence and self-esteem required to make her own decisions in her own way. You can too.

demeter
greek grain goddess of fertility

No seed sprouted in the rich soil, for bright crowned
      Demeter lay hidden;
Oxen in vain dragged the bent ploughs through the fields,
And white barley was scattered without avail on the ground.
By terrible famine she would have destroyed the
       whole race of men.
Homer, *Hymn to Demeter, c.* seventh century B.C.E.

After Persephone had been abducted by her uncle, Hades, Demeter refused to eat, drink, sleep, or wash until the girl was found. After nine days Demeter was at last told of her daughter's fate and she begged Zeus for Persephone's return. Less than sympathetic, Zeus told his sister to just accept her new son-in-law. Outraged, and with a bitter sense of betrayal, Demeter wandered through the land until she reached the town of Eleusis, near Athens, where, disguised as an old woman, she found work nursing a new baby.

Demeter brought up the boy, named Demophoon, as if he were a god, feeding him ambrosia and holding him nightly in the Fire of Immortality. But before he could be fully transformed, his mother stumbled upon Demeter's ritual and, fearing that the nurse was burning the boy, screamed out. Some stories say that upon hearing the cry Demeter dropped the boy, causing his death; others that she merely took the opportunity to reveal her true identity and commanded that a temple be built in her name. Thus, Eleusis became the center of a fertility cult and Demeter continued to be worshipped there up to the nineteenth century, although Christians frowned upon the overt sexuality of the annual springtime rites.

With Demeter away and neglecting her duties as Grain Goddess, the Earth underwent a famine. Exasperated at having his pleas to restore order ignored, Zeus finally commanded Hades to return Persephone to her mother. And she was, but for only part of the year, and when the new Queen of the Underworld returned to her husband, Demeter mourned once more, bringing about the winter, when nothing grows and all is dark and bleak.

olympian lineage

The second child of Rhea and Chronos, Demeter was sister to Hera (see pp. 84–89), Hestia, Hades, Poseidon, and Zeus, by whom she produced her only child, Persephone (see pp. 56–61). Like all her other siblings, Demeter was swallowed whole by her Titan father, who was chief of all the gods until he was overthrown by his youngest son, Zeus.

Symbols
* Horn of plenty – abundance of Demeter's harvest
* Wheat and sickle – representing the secrets of agriculture

Theme The empty nester
Key role Nurturing Mother
Life lesson Nothing gained is ever lost; separation is the precursor for reunion

Qualities

Functional	Dysfunctional
Earth mother	Overly protective
Nurturing	Self-neglecting
Strong maternal instinct	Narrow thinking
Generous	Uncompromising
Persistent	Needs to maintain status quo

present-day demeter

No sooner has the contemporary Demeter found a partner than she desired to be a mother. Bearing and bringing up children is her principal focus, frequently at great cost to herself and her relationship with their father. Many of us know mothers who put their children first and, when they leave home, find to their dismay that they no longer have a wifely role either.

The Demeter story illustrates the power of the maternal love bond. When betrayed by the Olympians, she unleashes her destructive side. In this patriarchally developed story, female power is thus defined as something negative, vengeful, and to be feared. This is another multifaceted tale, speaking metaphorically of the natural cycles of growth and death in agriculture and human life, plus of the loss that must precede a reunion.

The modern-day Demeter is the empty nester – the mother who has invested so much of herself in her offspring that, when they leave their childhood home, she is devastated at the resultant loss of identity and is unable to think or act in any positive, practical way.

However, the daughter's sexual initiation also offers the mother an opportunity for transformation and for their relationship to be reborn as equal, mutually enriching and intimate in a way that was not possible before, since the daughter had not shared the same life experience. The key for the Demeter archetype is to recognize the value of that separation and how much is to be gained from it. She must learn to give up the desire for power and domination over her daughter and welcome her as a peer.

This was very much the case with my own mother and the transformation of our relationship, once I had children of my own, was quite dramatic. For the first time we began to talk as women, which I found embraced wider and more intimate kinds of conversations than had been the case when we were just mother and daughter. It started with her imparting her wisdom about pregnancy, childbirth, and child-rearing. Then, as we settled into our new roles as women with shared experiences, we found we could open up to each other. I discovered my mother has a wonderful sense of humor, is a sensual being, and great fun to be with. Looking back I realize that it was only when my mother was prepared to relinquish her authority over me, stop treating me as her child, and interact as a peer that our relationship could develop in this way. It was like finding out that your boss is actually a real human being after all. Some people who are daughters may have always enjoyed this level of sharing and intimacy, but it is not so readily available to those with mothers who are in the hold of a strong Demeter archetype.

While the maternal nature of a strongly driven Demeter woman can never be assuaged, that desire can be positively redirected into professional or public life – whether as a counselor, mentor, or therapist. Thus she can find her later years as psychologically fulfilling and meaningful as her earlier ones.

How to develop Demeter
* Set aside some quiet, undisturbed time.
* Sit comfortably before your altar and relax. Let the objects inspire you.
* Light a scented candle or some incense to create a contemplative atmosphere.
* Center down until you reach a state of calm receptivity, breathing deeply and regularly.
* Focus on the questions or issues you wish to explore. Let your inner wisdom and creativity get to work.
* Afterward, record your discoveries and insights in your journal.

Demeter visualization exercise
One of the key challenges for Demeter women to face is their need for others to be dependent on them because they have spent so little time developing other facets of their lives. Thus the tendency to, even subconsciously, control and direct their children's lives long after it is appropriate. The following visualization will help balance such behavior with a sense of mutuality toward those you care for, and give full expression to all the many gifts you possess.

1. Lie or sit down. Dim the lighting, play soft music, and light scented candles. Close your eyes and let out a deep sigh. Breathe in deeply, hold, and then expel fully. Repeat twice.
2. Imagine you are looking at a box divided into nine sections. Each section represents a facet of your life and needs to be labeled. One of these sections relates to your children, another to your relationship with your spouse, and the rest to any paid work you do, your social life, hobbies and activities, your health, spiritual life and religious involvement, community commitments, etc. Imagine you are labeling each section now.

3. Revisit each compartment in turn. How full is each one, and with what? Consider the relative importance of the compartments – which part of your life dominates the middle? Which the outer areas?
4. Turn your attention to another box, which has only one compartment, full of toys, representing your children. Imagine that all those toys are taken away. What are you left with? An empty box. Could the same be said of the first box? Can you see how vulnerable you become when one important area of your life takes up all your time and attention?

hera
greek goddess of marriage

You were born together and together you shall be
    forever more...
But let there be spaces in your togetherness.
And let the winds of heaven dance between you.
Kahlil Gibran, *The Prophet*

With her strong desire to nurture, the young goddess Hera took pity on a tiny, wet, shivering bird, little realizing, until too late, that this was Zeus in disguise. The Chief God, having been married several times already and with a reputation as a seducer of goddesses and humans alike, had been pursuing the beautiful Hera for some time, without success. Only when he promised to marry her did she allow him near her. The marriage was not a success. Hera, a proud and jealous woman with a strong sex drive, was constantly betrayed by Zeus and his promiscuous ways. But instead of directing her anger at him, she took revenge on the other women.

Despite conceiving three children by Zeus and another, Hephaestus, who was born out of her thigh, Hera is not noted for her maternal instincts. Seeing that Hephaestus had been born with a club foot, she had him removed from Mount Olympus. This act marked Hera's bitterness at having produced a "deformed" child in contrast with Zeus' perfect daughter, Athena (see pp. 64–65), who had sprung from his head. Hera was not idle after each humiliation. Her vindictiveness required many of Zeus' illegitimate children to be banished and his lovers turned into beasts. Finally, worn down by Zeus' unrelenting betrayal, Hera left him and returned to her birthplace, the island of Samos. Rather than pursue his wife, which Zeus had the good sense to know would no longer work, he sent word that he was to marry again. Hera found him standing on a mountain alongside a veiled female statue. Amused, Hera was reconciled with Zeus. Their separation had helped her reconnect with her inner power and, having regained her independence and self-esteem, Hera found it easier to accept Zeus and love him unconditionally. The cold, dead statue only served to demonstrate how his dalliances had meant nothing to him compared with his love for her.

olympian lineage

Hera was sister to Demeter, Hestia, Hades, Poseidon, and Zeus, who was also her husband, and all were the children of Rhea and Chronos. She was a major figure in the Greek Pantheon, though most stories about her concern her stormy marriage to Zeus. The most well-known temple dedicated to her was the Heraion at Argos and she is most closely associated with the themes of marriage and fertility. Hellenic myth portrays Hera as her husband's inferior, but she is seen as an important goddess in her own right, who would have been seen as honoring Zeus by selecting him as her consort.

Symbols

* The peacock – a regal bird whose tail feather "eyes" reflect Hera's ever-watchful nature
* The sacred cow – provider of nourishment
* Intertwined gold rings – symbol of commitment and partnership

Theme — Marriage as a sacred, spiritual union

Key role — Faithful wife

Life lesson — Delaying partnership until you have explored the alignment of values with your partner; entering relationships with the head as well as the heart

Other roles

* Consort of Zeus, leader of the Olympians
* Vindictive, quarrelsome, and shrewish wife
* "Great Lady," her name being the female form of the Greek "hero"

Qualities	
Functional	Dysfunctional
Regal	Jealous
Powerful	Vindictive
Supportive	Quarrelsome
Needs commitment	Denies partner's faults
Dedicated homemaker	Puts partner first

present-day hera

In the same way that Demeter women desperately want to have children, a strong Hera archetype yearns to be a wife. This is a woman who, as a child, plays "husbands and wives," loves to dress up as a bride, and spends idle moments scribbling her name, the surname changed to whichever boy she is dating at the time.

An early, and usually very elaborate, wedding follows, the need to be married overriding any suggestion that perhaps the couple should first get to know each other a little better. A Hera woman cannot understand why anyone wants to remain single. Not one for having many female friends anyway, she is the woman who steers her husband well away from unattached ladies at parties. For her, marriage is a life-long, sacred commitment and Heaven protect any partner who does not share that view. Because of her utter dependence on her husband, particularly in terms of the status he confers on her, the Hera wife will not risk confronting him with his infidelities. The "other woman" is always to blame. Unlike her Demeter sister, who is too involved with her children to care, the Hera archetype will always get her revenge.

In its dysfunctional form this archetype highlights the addictive personality – someone in love with the idea of marriage, who makes her choice solely on the basis of emotion and with little or no rational thought involved. A Hera personality needs to learn to cultivate discernment in her choices – particularly with regard to shared values. The exercise on page 89 demonstrates how.

Shared values are perhaps the single most important aspect of a partnership. When we are more concerned with the external aspects of a relationship, such as the status that marriage confers upon us, the kudos brought by a partner's "important" job or how much he earns, there is a tendency to ignore how such partnerships must serve deeper, inner needs. However, it is crucial for our long-term happiness and in order to cultivate a truly spiritual bond, that we examine the extent to which our values are shared by our partners, and vice versa. Values are difficult to define precisely, but essentially they are the guiding principles that underpin every attitude we hold, the behavior we exhibit, and every single action we decide to take. Such values affect every part of our lives – from our attitudes about openness and honesty within relationships to what loyalty, duty, respect, integrity, fairness, and passion mean to us. The one area where couples frequently discover that their values do not match is when they have children and deep-seated, deeply felt values inherited from their own upbringings re-emerge.

Because Hera women are usually so eager to marry, and are often more in love with the institution itself than the person they choose, there is a risk they will, after the honeymoon, discover that they and their spouses actually have very little in common. Hera, the goddess placed a high value on fidelity; her husband did not. Facing such attitudes and values squarely before the wedding, rather than imagining they can change the other person afterwards, saves Hera archetypes a great deal of pain and distress.

How to develop Hera

* Set aside some quiet, undisturbed time.
* Sit comfortably before your altar and relax. Let the objects inspire you.
* Light a scented candle or some incense to create a contemplative atmosphere.
* Center down until you reach a state of calm receptivity, breathing deeply and regularly.
* Focus on the questions or issues you wish to explore. Let your inner wisdom and creativity get to work.
* Afterward, record your discoveries and insights in your journal.

How to decide what is important

Complete each of the following sentences as honestly as you can. The aim is to write down only what is important to you.

* Love means …
* Relationships are …
* A wife is …
* A husband is …
* I expect … from our relationship
* Power is …
* The most important thing in my life is …

1. If possible, ask your partner to answer these questions separately, then compare what each of you has written. If this is not feasible, then imagine that your partner is sitting with you and that you are asking him to complete these sentences. What do you feel he would say? Note here that I have written "feel," not "think." Allow your heart to guide you toward honest answers – trust your intuition to help you.

2. What do you conclude? To what extent are your values about relationships in alignment? How far are they polarized? Any partnership involves compromise and it is as undesirable to live with a clone of yourself as it is to be with someone whose view of reality is utterly different from your own. Therefore, be quite clear which of your values are core guiding principles – that is, which of them are "nonnegotiable." For example, if like Hera a core value is fidelity and your partner does not consider this important, you will need to discuss how that might affect your degree of trust in him.

3. Within organizations it is said that there has to be a certain number of values in alignment in order for those businesses to succeed. The same is true of other partnerships, including personal ones. If you and your partner place similar importance on certain key principles and life decisions – whether to have children, how you treat each other in company, or the balance between the rest of your life and work – then you are likely to travel your journey together in a mutually satisfying way. If there is too much incongruity between you, then expect a bumpy ride.

Affirmations

* Even within my partnership I retain my own identity
* I recognize the importance of being discerning about my partner's qualities
* The greater the integration between all the many parts of myself, the less I need to look for a partner to complete me
* I now reclaim my power in this relationship and in so doing am taking the first steps toward honoring myself
* My needs are just as important as my partner's
* I willingly take responsibility for all parts of my life
* Whatever the circumstances, I am ruler of my own destiny

gaia
the earth goddess

According to the pagan version of Big Bang Theory, in the beginning the chaotic void produced the Deep-Breasted One, Gaia, the earliest of divinities. It is she who was worshipped at Delphi before Apollo's followers usurped her temple. She had such widespread influence that the new patriarchy continued to adhere to the laws of the Mother Goddess. Gaia is associated with Isis in Egypt, the Canaan goddess Astarte, Sumerian-Babylonian deity Tiamat, Mesopotamia's Mama, and the Hindu's Kali Ma (see pp. 98–103), all of whom were worshipped as part of the universal matriarchal religion between 3000 and 1000 B.C.E.

Hesiod informs us that Gaia appeared out of Chaos and gave birth to Ouranos, or Uranus, the starlit sky. Gaia then slept with Uranus to produce the Titans, the "ancestors of humankind." Each of the deities produced by Gaia, Uranus, and their progeny symbolize the various forces of Nature or abstract human qualities.

Present-day Gaia
* Having a deep abiding belief in the rightful place of woman as Creatrix
* Feeling strong connection with the Earth as a living entity
* Comfortable with change and uncertainty – chaos being the precursor of Gaia
* Toying with the idea of having a child by an unknown donor
* Being in tune with the Triple Goddess – Maiden, Mother, and Wise Woman

Functional qualities

Completeness/Wholeness
Generosity/Abundance
The embodiment of love
Energy

Visual themes

* Temple at Delphi
* Goddess of Willendorf
* Earth as a womb
* Joining of Heaven and Earth
* Breasts and pregnancy
* Depiction of Chronos or Time
* Feasting

Developing Gaia

1. Decide to spend time by your-self, thus forming a relationship with yourself.

2. Commit to experiencing Nature fully, in whatever form it is avail-able to you. Be aware of the changing colors of leaves and sky, the fragrances of different flow-ers, the textures of wood, the sounds of the countryside.

3. Meditate upon what love means to you. It was Gaia's desire for love that caused her to create her son, Ouranos, the Heavens.

4. Explore how connected you feel with everything around you.

Be open to the concept of one single, pulsating energy mass that inextricably links everything and everyone upon this planet.

5. Reflect on the extent to which you act upon your intuition, that ineffable connection with all that ever has been, is, or will be. Gaia's temple at Delphi celebrated her all-knowing nature.

6. Consider how you might fur-ther direct your energy through creative enterprises and greater productivity. Gaia was a strong, fertile force who produced count-less offspring. What have you given birth to recently?

amaterasu
the sun goddess

The Sun Goddess, Amaterasu Omikami, is the only female chief divinity of a contemporary religion, in this case Shinto, the official religion of Japan since before Buddhism was introduced from China in the sixth century. The circle on the Japanese flag represents a mirror, one of the religion's three sacred treasures, which Amaterasu is said to have given to her grandson Ninigi-no Mikoto, when he descended from Heaven to govern Earth. The goddess' instructions were that it was to be kept in the Imperial Palace, home of the Japanese emperor, considered to be directly descended from the Shinto deities. According to Shinto, there is no polarized good and evil in the world, simply appropriateness and wrongness. Therefore, acting angrily toward someone who is doing you a bad deed is acceptable, while doing so just because you are feeling out of sorts at the time is inappropriate and unjustified.

Present-day Amaterasu
* Placing high value on authentic and appropriate behavior
* Recognizing that our external lives are reflections of our inner worlds
* Demonstrating balance and grace within our own life and taking joy in that of others
* Liking to maintain a sense of order in all things
* Generally taking a positive approach to challenging situations

Functional qualities

Clarity

Graciousness

Balance

Orderliness

Positiveness

Goodness

Visual themes

∗ The red circle of the Japanese flag
∗ The sun: she is a solar goddess
∗ The Imperial Palace
∗ Her three sacred treasures – the mirror, a bejeweled necklace and a sword

Developing Amaterasu

1. Look into a mirror in candle-light and honestly examine what you see. What does your appearance tell you about the state of your spirit? What does gazing into your own eyes tell you about your Higher Self? Reflect on how you can modify yourself within to improve external circumstances. For example, if you find that other people do not respect you, con-sider how far you are respectful of yourself. If you are lonely, become your own best friend.

2. Meditate on how far your life is balanced and orderly. Do you pay greater attention to health, friendships, and spiritual devel-opment, rather than partnerships and work, for example? Would a course in time management help you alleviate stress and frustrations?

3. Think about ways in which you can pour more sunshine into your life. What gives you the greatest pleasure? Stop looking to others to bring you joy, do these things for yourself. Make a list of seven things, one for every day of the week, that would fill your life with light – from buying yourself flowers to preparing yourself a wonderful candlelit dinner or complimenting yourself on all your attributes and achievements.

wise woman

5

It is no coincidence that I began early menopause while concluding this book. This third section troubled me, since I would have been uncomfortable writing about something of which I had no personal knowledge. But here I find myself, relatively young, experiencing night sweats, hot flashes, and mood swings. Despite having longed to see the end of menstruation, the transition to Wise Woman has not been as straightforward as I assumed it would be, but I feel I can now write about this rite of passage in a much more authentic way.

It is part of the process of being human to grieve over what has been lost. The ending of periods, plus associated physical and psychological signs, brought aging home to me. Although I have never been obsessed with my appearance I nonetheless found that I could not avoid mourning the death of the Maiden and Mother, and only reluctantly welcome the Wise Woman, or Crone. Then I saw a delightful film called

Harold and Maude, which explores the relationship between two unlikely lovers. Harold is a rich young man, who dismisses the vacuous girls his mother introduces him to. Maude is the old lady with a glint in her eye, joy in her heart, and a childlike view of the world, who captures his heart. What this story illustrates is key to our understanding of the Wise Woman archetype. Maude is attractive to Harold because of her energy, her sense of wonderment and adventure, her *joie de vivre* – all compelling, sexy qualities that are not the exclusive property of the young. Therein lies the key to embracing the Wise Woman. It is about having the best of both worlds – all that life-experience and self-knowledge combined with the freedom of speech and action. After all, no one is going to tell you to keep your opinions to yourself because you do not know what you are talking about as they may have done when you were a child. They wouldn't dare. This is not about an ending, but a beginning. It is not about not caring what others think of you, but living your life according to your own values, in your own way.

It is hoped that you have at least one Wise Woman role model to teach you that age is not something to be feared. Getting older offers us an opportunity to reexplore our lives from a wiser perspective and to enjoy new-found freedoms. The Wise Woman goddesses are perhaps the most challenging to identify with because they represent both destruction and creation. This is one of the great paradoxes of life. Light and dark, good and evil, masculine and feminine are complementary. How can you appreciate good health unless you have been ill? How can you know true love if you have not experienced rejection? Yet the Wise Woman archetype encourages you to look beyond. To question why we attribute certain characteristics to things, why some actions are "good," others "bad." If you consider the different perspectives from various cultures, you will realize that concepts of

good or bad, what is acceptable or unacceptable, are socially constructed. There is no universal reality, only the definitions that we attribute to certain things. And we can change our minds about them any time we choose.

What the Wise Woman offers us is the freedom to reappraise our view of the world, to see that Kali Ma, ceaseless destroyer of demons, is also saving the world through her actions. Who is to say that her methods are unacceptable? By what authority do we judge her? When we accept the shadow side of human nature – then we become more accepting, compassionate, and forgiving. We become non-judgmental, the first stage of our liberation. The wisdom of the Crone allows you to see the world with new eyes and question "right" and "wrong," exchanging those judgments by accepting "what is."

Writing about the menopause, Leslie Kenton calls this stage a "call to adventure" and it is no surprise that women become writers, artists, and business-women at this time. But this new power is also about spiritual issues. This completes the female trinity – the Virgin concerned with physicality and the body, the Mother having introduced us to the psychological, emotional, and mental, and the Wise Woman rediscovering her core self deep in her soul, learning to live according to the spirit. It is not surprising, then, that patriarchy, by focusing on the external and superficial, has feared the Dark Goddess and imposed its distorted mind-set and values on her stories. But, if you explore these fairy tales with an open mind, you will find that the witch, or shadow, was the catalyst for self-change. Without her influence there would be no happy ending. So, regardless of age, I urge you to shun the male-dominant world view with its prurient messages about women and their bodies. Take back your freedom and power. Embrace the Dark Goddess and recognize her for the companion, mentor, and guardian she is.

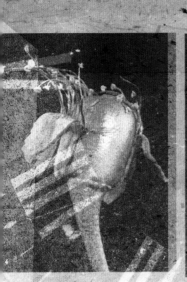
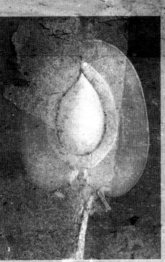

The creator–destroyer
The archetypes of the Wise Woman are perhaps the most challenging in the goddess firmament. This is because they represent both the creative and the destructive aspects of life and human nature as a continuum. Each is an aspect of the other, without which we cannot exist.

kali ma
hindu goddess (or devi) of birth and death

She stands on the bosom of her consort, Shiva;
It is because She is the Shakti, the Power,
Inseparable from the Absolute. She is
Surrounded by jackals and other unholy creatures,
    the denizens of the cremation ground.
But is not the Ultimate reality above holiness and
    unholiness?
The Gospel of Sri Ramakrishna, nineteenth-century Hindu saint

With her black face leering over the body of her consort, Shiva, his bloody entrails dripping from her mouth and a necklace of skulls jangling, the Hindu Goddess Kali Ma is a terrifying sight. She is the ultimate Shadow figure, representing polarities that the western mind finds difficult to accommodate in one being. Although many tales associated with Kali seem horribly violent, she also inspires beautiful and loving poetry. She is the quintessential enigma.

Kali is said to have been born when masculine values dominated human existence and indeed the Brahmans, members of the highest Hindu caste, even devolved her triple attributes to three male gods: Brahma as Creator, Vishnu as Preserver, and Shiva as Destroyer. But many Hindu scriptures, including the Nirvana Tantra, dismissed this attempt at subjugating Kali's importance and stayed loyal to the One Primordial Being, the Mother of the World.

Kali sprang from the third eye of Durga, a fierce Warrior Goddess, who was trying to rid the world of the vicious demons that had captured humanity. Armed with ferocious weapons and a laugh that could chill blood, she ripped her enemies into pieces, drinking their blood. On one occasion she became so drunk that she began to dance wildly until she realized that the flesh beneath her feet belonged to Shiva, and that she was trampling him to death. It is said that one day Kali Ma will resume her dance and bring an end to the world.

Kali's favorite method of killing demons was to behead them and for centuries in India, male human sacrifices, through decapitation, were offered to the Goddess.

hindu lineage

Kali Ma is the most malignant aspect of the goddess Sakti, and possibly the most frightening aspect of the Great Goddess. Her consort is usually thought of as Shiva, whom she abets in his negative aspects. Some myths represent her as the personified anger and ferociousness of the powerful goddess Durga. Nirtti, Goddess of Darkness is also associated with Kali.

Symbols

Kali's sacred colors – or Gunas – linked to her triple forms:
* Virgin – white – birth
* Mother – red – life
* Crone – black – death

Theme	The impermanence of life
Key role	Creator and destroyer
Life lesson	Only when we let go of old ways of being is our world transformed and our true potential finally fulfilled

Other Kali Ma roles
* Black Mother Time
* Terrible Mother
* Savior of the world
  (from evil demons)

Qualities	
Functional	Dysfunctional
Creative	Destructive
Protective	Vengeful
Power-giving	Devouring
Free	Fierce
Tolerant	Wild

present-day kali ma

You may feel that a Goddess who devours flesh and dances on bloodless corpses is an archetype that has little relevance to you. In order to find any application it is important to look beyond the bloody imagery and explore the essential Kali Ma. Whether we accept it or not, there is a part of her in all of us. The challenge facing us before we can truly embody the wisdom of the Dark Mother, is to shake off our lifelong cultural and religious baggage. To welcome, as Kant put it, the death of Dogma and hence the birth of Reality, indeed, to look at the world once again through fresh eyes.

One of the questions I frequently ask myself when faced with difficult situations is: "What if this were all all right?" Too often we exacerbate particular scenarios by judging how things should or should not be. We make assumptions about other people's motives and jump to conclusions in an all-too-negative way. Women who have developed a strong Kali Ma archetype are frequently found shrugging their shoulders, saying "Perhaps" to others' inferences, and waiting patiently until they have all the pieces of

life's jigsaw puzzle instead of guessing what the "big picture" might be or mean. Once you start questioning why you have certain beliefs you may be startled to find that your whole life has been based on meanings imposed by others – from parents and teachers to the media and religious leaders. That is not freedom – and certainly not the freedom enjoyed by a Wise Woman.

We may initially be appalled at Kali Ma because violence, death, and destruction are not considered female traits. Yet, paradoxically, Mother Nature is the most violent and destructive force there is, unleashing earthquakes, storms, and volcanic eruptions against which humans are powerless to protect themselves.

Because the patriarchal order chose not to comprehend or respect the Feminine Principle, but remained fearful of it, Kali's metaphorical images have been grossly misunderstood and maligned. Her "gory" flesh-eating, blood-consuming dance simply represents how life is a never-ending cycle of endings and beginnings, death and rebirth. The concept of flesh and blood as an elixir of immortality pervades many early philosophies and religions. Even Christians embrace this concept through drinking wine and eating a wafer (symbolizing Christ's blood and body) at Holy Communion.

Embracing the Kali Ma archetype encourages us to acknowledge the Terrible Mother – the dark, culturally repressed side that must exist in all of us to complement the light the Lucifer in us that serves to help us better understand the Divine within. She also causes us to realize that there is much that is not vulnerable to death and that everything else is just an illusion. To achieve true wisdom requires eliminating everything we once held dear. The search for wisdom can only commence when we begin to doubt. Doubt is the catalyst for the sort of qualitative change of mind-set that leads to transformation and is the legacy of Kali Ma.

How to develop Kali Ma

* Set aside some quiet, undisturbed time.
* Sit comfortably before your altar and relax. Let the objects inspire you.
* Light a scented candle or some incense to create a contemplative atmosphere.
* Center down until you reach a state of calm receptivity, breathing deeply and regularly.
* Focus on the questions or issues you wish to explore. Let your inner wisdom and creativity get to work.
* Afterward, record your discoveries and insights in your journal.

Assumption-busting exercise

Just as a journey seems harder the closer you get to the end, so the passage to the Wise Woman is a particularly challenging one, and especially with regard to the Kali Ma archetype. This not an easy exercise, but it is abundantly worthwhile. Try it for just ten minutes a day, then one hour, then several days… and so on. Start by repeating the following affirmation to yourself, as often as needed:

"I commit to making no judgment or assumptions about whatever happens in the next (few minutes/hours/day)."

As the German writer and polymath, Goethe (1749–1832) said, once you commit to something, then Providence moves too. All you have to do is to look for one, two, or more alternative meanings to whatever occurs in your life over a given period of time. For example, what options are available to you if you have only one lemon and two people ask you for it? Would you cut it in half so they could share it? Or should one of them find another lemon? Or should they toss a coin for it?

Yet saying anything at all is the opposite of the wisdom that is accumulated by embracing the Wise Woman archetype. What is required is questioning rather than jumping to conclusions. In the lemon example the Wise Woman would ask the two people why they each need a lemon in the first place. Only when you have this information can you hope to provide the right solution. If one needs juice for a drink and the other peel for a cake, then both can be satisfied by one lemon.

Commit, today, to stop applying meanings to things. Ask questions that will help you uncover the myriad significances that can be discerned from even the smallest event. And then, when you have a selection of answers to choose from, use your intuition and wisdom to select one that seems right for you.

cailleach
celtic goddess of war, death, and sovereignty

She crouched like a wild beast ready to spring
She of the long nails, she of the long teeth
She ran through the hills like thunder.
Scottish folk song

The term *cailleach* means "hag," "old woman," or "the veiled one," alluding to her destructive power as the bringer of death. It also means "nun," an interesting definition coming from a time when paganism and Christianity were battling for the hearts, minds, and souls of the populace. Like Kali Ma, with whom she is closely associated, the Cailleach had a gruesome appearance – gray hair "like brushwood in a dying forest" framing a blue-black face, with a single eye and solitary red tooth. She is the epitome of the ugly old hag, the protagonist of fairy tales and that which women fear becoming; the reason why the concept of the Crone is so challenging to embrace.

Already commonly worshipped when the Celts arrived in Ireland and Scotland some 2,000 years ago, reverence for the Cailleach never died out. However, because of her antiquity little is known of this seasonal goddess. We do know that she represents winter and is constantly battling with younger adversaries, the spring deities who age and wither in time, resulting again in the powerful sovereignty of the hag.

In some stories the Cailleach has an insatiable sexual energy and finds young men with whom to take her pleasure before discarding them. While they age and die, she remains unchanged. The myths also tell of her immense strength: working on her farm, carrying boulders in her apron, and even moving mountains. Many rocky features are named after her, such as the Hag Hills, or Beinn na Chailleach, in Scotland.

Both creative and destructive, a theme common to the Wise Woman archetype, the Caillech is said to control the weather, bringing about or withholding fierce storms, high winds, and freezing temperatures.

celtic lineage

This mysterious, ancient Celtic goddess, appearing alternately as either a hag or a beautiful maiden, gives her name to Scotland, originally known as Caledonia. While common to Irish and Scottish folklore, it is from the southwest of Ireland that this myth is believed to have originated. It is possible that she is a pre-Celtic divinity. As Cailleach Bearra she appears in the ninth-century *Lament of the Old Woman of Beare*, a monologue recalling the days of her youth and her present solitary old age. Like Hecate, she pursues young men.

Symbol
Spinning wheel – sometimes referred to as the Spinning Hag, the Cailleach was sent to torment women on their inability to spin amounts of unusual substances into fine thread, punishing them for their failures.

Theme	Reclamation of personal power
Key role	Female guardian of the wild
Life lesson	Your sovereignty lies in your ability to embrace insularity; to need no one's adoration but your own self-love.

Other Cailleach roles
* Black Mother (with whom she is linked with Kali Ma, see pp. 98–103)
* Spirit of Disease
* Black Queen – the Spanish Califia, after whom California is named

Qualities	
Functional	Dysfunctional
Inner strength	Manipulative
Unmaterialistic	Ruthless
High self-esteem	Stern/cold
Creative	Destructive
Powerful	Vindictive

present-day cailleach

The Cailleach manifests herself in all those women who are uncon-cerned and completely secure about their outward appearance. They are the ones who are sometimes called "wild," though this does not reflect the character beneath the external shell. The Cailleach type is also the one who has learned the difference between solitariness and loneliness. She considers her insularity and aloneness to be a sign of power, rather than a personal failing; she has moved beyond the need for societal approbation.

Having spent the requisite time getting to know herself, this archetype is now strong and confident, perhaps not nec-essarily physically but certainly emotionally and psychologically. However, living as we do in a society with a particular set of values, one in which the Wise Woman, or Crone, has been denigrated in stories for centuries, Cailleach must beware of being considered detached and distant. The crucial factor, as with all things, is to be happy to be on one's own, but to welcome friendship, too.

The Cailleach manifests herself in women who are uncon-cerned with outward appearance. The ones who confidently ignore the beauty industry's obsession with covering every strand of gray

and eradicating every wrinkle. Clothes are chosen for comfort not fashion. While these women defy all entreaties to conform to patriarchal society's idea of what an attractive woman should look like, they are usually of great interest to men. There is something indefinably seductive about a woman who is so *together*. Cailleach women are the ones who have learned the difference between being comfortable with solitude and enduring loneliness. They consider their insularity to be a sign of power – they have moved beyond the need for societal approbation. Having spent time getting to know herself, this archetype is strong emotionally and psychologically. She is comfortable in her own skin and fully accepts herself.

It is likely that the Cailleach will only become a strong archetype in your life when you have worked through a period of solitude, frequently after the death of a spouse. Once you have grieved and accepted being alone you discover that you have to lose yourself in order to find yourself again. However, the Cailleach must beware of being perceived as cold as the season she is believed to have controlled. The key is balance: to be comfortable with one's own company but to welcome the people who want to offer companionship. To pursue one's own interests while being mindful of the needs of others. To know when it is all right to take time for oneself while being aware of the importance of participating fully in this world.

How to develop Cailleach
* Set aside some quiet, undisturbed time.
* Sit comfortably before your altar and relax. Let the objects inspire you.
* Light a scented candle or some incense to create a contemplative atmosphere.
* Center down until you reach a state of calm receptivity, breathing deeply and regularly.
* Focus on the questions or issues you wish to explore. Let your inner wisdom and creativity get to work.
* Afterward, record your discoveries and insights in your journal.

Affirmations
* I am becoming my own best friend.
* I am learning to love my life exactly as it is; as long as I know myself truly I will never be alone.
* I am becoming less dependent on others for my sense of self-worth.
* My goal is to live life to the fullest, drawing pleasure from every moment.
* With every passing year I am becoming more confident about who I am and how important I am to the Universe.

Insularity exercise

You are about to plan a very special outing for someone. This is a person you love very much but perhaps have been out of touch with for a while. You therefore want to give this person an experience he/she will never forget. As it happens, this person has exactly the same tastes and desires as you. In fact, it is you – that part of yourself that Jung calls "the Shadow," the Dark Goddess that resides within your soul.

Take a sheet of paper and write down all the things that your inner self, your Shadow self, would love to have prepared for an evening when the two of you are completely alone. The only rules are that there should be no intrusion from the outside world, which means no television, radio, or other stimuli such as magazines. You might like to think about how your choices relate to the various facets of yourself:

* What can you do for your body?
* What can you do for your mind?
* What can you do for your emotions?
* What can you do to inspire your spirit?

Here is a sample answer:

* Preparing and eating a sumptuous meal of my favorite foods – three courses – all served on my best china and silverware, with candles and proper napkins
* Listening to my favorite music
* Flicking through a selection of favorite books
* Massaging my arms and legs with wonderfully scented aromatherapy oils
* Being completely naked all evening – having the heat turned up really high
* Jumping up and down on the bed, having a pillow fight against the wall
* Putting on a tape of someone laughing and joining in, until tears run down my face
* Finally, when my senses have had their fill, sitting and gazing into the middle distance, doing absolutely nothing.

Think of as many things as possible that you can do for yourself during this one special time – either an evening or on the weekend. Possibilities are limitless. Just remember to make a commitment to enjoy the company you have by shutting out the rest of the world; do not answer the telephone or the door. Gather together everything you need in advance.

There are several things you could experience

1. You hated being by yourself. Explore what made it so unpleasant. If you can't enjoy your own company, how can anyone else? Did you really dream up all the things that you feel passionate about? Did you hold back from totally treating yourself, and how does that withholding creep in to other aspects of your life?

2. You were surprised how much you enjoyed being by yourself and intend to repeat this exercise again in the future, coming up with even more inventive ways to delight your "Shadow."

3. Because you normally live by yourself normally and have always considered yourself an insular person, you had forgotten how important it is to really be good to yourself. It is not enough just to exist. What life demands from us is to really "be" – to nurture our minds, bodies, and spirits, so that we are constantly experiencing the very best we can be.

hecate
goddess of the dark moon

The Moon is Hecate, Her power appears in three forms,
Having as symbol of the new moon the figure
    in the while robe
And golden sandals, and torches lighted;
The basket which she bears when she has mounted high is
    the symbol of the cultivation of the crops which she
    made to grow up according to the increase of her light.
Porphyry (c. 234-305 A.D.) , Neoplatonist, scholar and philosopher

Hecate's story is closely linked with both Persephone (see pp. 56–61) and Demeter (see pp. 78–83). It is Hecate who tells the frantic mother that she had heard Persephone's screams as she was being abducted by Hades, and suggests that they go to find out more from Helios, the Sun God. He fills in the details, having watched the scene, and informs Demeter that Zeus himself had sanctioned the rape. In addition, Hecate becomes Persephone's companion after the Maiden Goddess' first experience in the Underworld. Hence Hecate is a metaphor for an understanding of new dimensions of being and the gateway to fresh possibilities.

    Hecate's own story, illustrating how a heavenly Moon Goddess became associated with demons, sorcery, and magic, demonstrates the patriarchal order's desire to distance itself from the birth process. Hecate, finding herself in the house of a woman during childbirth, was forcibly plunged by the other gods into the River Acheron to wash away "contagious" traces. The current dragged Hecate into the Underworld, where she became Hades' wife. Strongly associated with female power, Hecate became demonized as Queen of the Witches, said to commune with evil spirits. It was through fear of this Goddess that so many midwives met their deaths during the persecutions of the late Middle Ages.

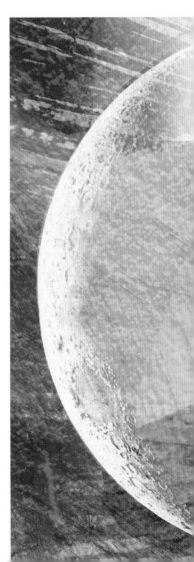

greek lineage

Hecate is linked with many other Greek goddesses as well as the Egyptian Midwife–Goddess Hekat, or Heket, who was said to be responsible for the delivery of the Sun God each morning, and was associated with the tribal matriarchy of predynastic Egypt. She represents the female trinity, variously in the form of Hebe the Virgin, Hera the Mother (see pp. 84–89), and Hecate the Crone. Some versions of the triad relate to Hecate Selene, the Heavenly Moon, Artemis the Earthly Huntress (see pp. 46–51) and Persephone, Queen of the Underworld.

Symbols
* The Moon
* The frog – symbol of the fetus (Hecate being strongly associated with midwives)

Theme	The magical power of the feminine principle
Key role	Wise witch
Life lesson	To get in touch with, and learn to trust, your intuition

Other Hecate roles
* Goddess of the Crossroads
* Goddess of the Mysterious, Sorcery, and Magic
* The Distant One, offering sage advice and guidance, particularly during the hours of darkness

Qualities	
Functional	Dysfunctional
Creative	Destructive
Intuitive	Ignoring
Protective	Manipulative
Transformative	Secretive
Mentoring	Distant

present-day hecate

In her functional form, the Hecate archetype is highly intuitive. She is comfortable with introspection and uses this to uncover ways in which to ensure that her day-to-day life is fulfilling and meaningful. Having been brought up in a society that fixates on the logical, the explicable, and the material, female intuition is frequently belittled, yet it is an attribute that is increasingly used in business. Many high-level entrepreneurs – both male and female – base their decisions on "gut feelings." This is particularly true when it comes to choosing people to work with. In most cases it is impossible to select one candidate over another purely on the basis of what you read in their curriculum vitae. The successful ones are those we feel we will "gel" with, who we can relate to on an emotional as well as a mental level. This information comes to us from our intuition.

Thus Hecate can help you approach decisions and actions from a deeper level, one that is more consistent with what your heart is directing you to do, than your mind. In this she is very different from the Goddess Athena (see pp. 64–65), who is rooted more in the cerebral. If you find yourself relating mostly to Athena, then invoking Hecate from time to time is a valuable exercise, so that you can consider what to do from both perspectives.

Hecate behavior

* Becoming more creative the older you get. This does not necessarily mean becoming a writer, painter, or craftsperson. Creativity also encompasses finding solutions to problems by making associations between things that seem unrelated
* Becoming drawn to mentoring or coaching younger women
* Increasingly trusting your intuition and confidently acting on your hunches despite others' focus on logical solutions

How to develop Hecate

* Set aside some quiet, undisturbed time.
* Sit comfortably before your altar and relax. Let the objects inspire you.
* Light a scented candle or some incense to create a contemplative atmosphere.
* Center down until you reach a state of calm receptivity, breathing deeply and regularly.
* Focus on the questions or issues you wish to explore. Let your inner wisdom and creativity get to work.
* Afterward, record your discoveries and insights in your journal.

Intuition exercise

1. Think about what issue or question you require answered, possibly one that your rational mind has been unable to solve. Phrase it in an open-ended way so as to not place any limitations on Universal Guidance, such as, "What do I need to know in order to take the proper action?"

2. Take a moment to calm yourself physically and mentally. Do whatever works for you to get yourself in a peaceful frame of mind. Don't rush this part. The more relaxed you are, the more you will be certain of operating only from the right hemisphere of your brain, the part concerned with intuition and creative approaches.

3. Now, while maintaining a relaxed focus, move around the room and, on impulse, pick up an object that you find lying there. (In another version of this exercise you may wish to collect items and place them on a table beforehand.) Trust that whatever you choose will be the right symbol that you need at this time. Always go with your first, instinctive response.

4. Examine your object carefully. Reflect on it from the perspective of its shape, color, size, weight, what it is, its potential, whether it is warm or cool to the touch, what it is made from. Write down all these characteristics.

5. When you've completed this list think about your original issue. How might any or all of these attributes relate to your problem? Remember that the Universe consists of infinite connections – all things are linked to each other, even if we cannot immediately see how. That is the mystery of creativity. Somewhere on your list will be the answer you need or the catalyst that will cause you to come up with an intuitive solution to your problem.

Affirmations

* My life experience is invaluable to others. I am happy to offer support and guidance to women whose life path is different mine
* Every day in every way I am becoming more creative – the associations I make are simply greater proof of the connections between all things in the Universe
* My intuition is an innate compass that draws me ever closer to personal happiness and fulfillment
* I have the power to transform my life in every moment

ceridwen
keeper of the cauldron of inspiration and knowledge

This Welsh mythical sorceress and goddess was keeper of the Cauldron of Inspiration and Knowledge. Her children were Crearwy, a daughter, whose name means "light" or "beautiful," and a son, Afagddu, meaning "dark" or "ugly." In order to compensate for Afagddu's disadvantages, Ceridwen began to brew a magical potion that would grant the boy total wisdom. However, she foolishly left a servant, Gwion, in charge of watching it boil for a year, the required amount of time for the magic to develop.

Three drops of the liquid fell on Gwion's hand and, unthinking, he licked them, assimilating all the knowledge intended for Afagddu for himself. A furious Ceridwen chased him across the land, shapeshifting from one animal or bird to another. Finally, Ceridwen metamorphosed into a hen and, having transformed Gwion into grains of corn, promptly ate him up. Nine months later the witch gave birth to Taliesin. Possessor of all knowledge and the gift of prophecy, Taliesin grew up to become a wonderful poet. He foretold the death of King Maelgwyn, a historical figure said to have died in 547 A.D.

Ceridwen behavior
* Being uncomfortable with or resisting your Shadow side
* Preferring to pass responsibility for self-development to others, for example to a "guru"
* Having failed to give yourself credit for your innate power and wisdom
* Remaining fearful of your power within

Visual themes
* Corpse-eating sow (the root Cerdo, from which her name comes, is Spanish for pig)
* Keeper of the magic cauldron
* Shapeshifter (from human to animal or bird and back again)

Dysfunctional qualities
Neglectful of responsibilities

Vengeful

Aspects for meditation
1. In what ways do you seek to overcompensate for your Shadow side (represented in the story by the dark Afagddu)?
2. If you were to brew a cauldron of wisdom, what would it contain? How many of these attributes do you possess and how many do you need to develop? How might you achieve them?
3. How do you abdicate responsibility for your power and wisdom? Who is the foolish servant in your life? What would you choose to do differently?
4. Consider the concept of shapeshifting, the power of wicca to bend or shape, to recreate. How far have you developed your innate ability to change your consciousness at will?
5. Destruction is necessary for rebirth. This is the way of Nature. Where in this life cycle are you currently? To what extent are you clear about what it is you want to give birth to?

hel
the norse queen of the underworld

Hel is the Norse Queen of the Underworld, who gave her name to the concept of "hell." In keeping with many of her Wise Woman "sisters," Hel was a fearsome-looking creature, whose role it was to receive all the dead into her domain, except for those who had died in battle. These unfortunates were transported to Valhalla, palace of Odin, by the Valkyries, Angels of Death, who hovered over battle-fields and whose leader, according to medieval legend, was called Brunnhilde ("Burning Hel").

Despite the deathly association, the Norse-Germanic cultures perceived Hel to be a benevolent goddess. Medieval titles heaped upon her include Lady of Abundance and Satiety. Her loyal followers were called Hallequins ("ladies of the night"), who promised prosperity to households in exchange for sustenance.

Hel is closely linked with Hecate (see pp.110–113) and is another Triple Goddess. She is a metaphor for the subconscious and inspired the womblike shrines dedicated to her in dark, sacred caves, which were often linked to underground volcanoes or steam vents, spreading the association of hell with intense heat.

The word "helmet" means magic mask, which northern shamans believed could render them invisible, in order that they might enter the Underworld and return to Earth without dying.

Hel behavior
* Connecting with your Shadow self through meditation or personal development work
* Strongly resisting the concept of hell and a punishing deity
* Coming to terms with mortality
* Developing the knack of becoming "invisible" in dangerous situations

Visual themes
* Bat – her companion creature
* Queen of the Underworld
* Dark or waning Moon
* Valkyries and Brunnhilde
* Fire as magical, purgative medium
* Associations with mountains and volcanoes
* Triple Goddess, related to the Greek Hecate

Functional qualities
Balanced

All-powerful supreme being

Acceptance of the shadow

Aspects for meditation

1. What associations do you make when you hear the word "hell?" How much of that has been informed by religious doctrine? Consider why a benevolent Universe would wish to impose external damnation on certain souls. What political agenda might have been responsible for this ideology?

2. Explore other cultures' views on death and what happens to our souls afterward.

3. To what extent are you comfortable facing your Shadow side? Do you avoid journeying into the subconscious because of what you fear you might find there? Might those terrifying figures be no more than things that, when brought into the light, seem to be harmless? Think about how, as a child, you may have been afraid of frightening shapes on a wall, but found in the morning that they were only your much-loved toys.

4. Visualize putting on your own helmet of invisibility whenever you engage in psychic work or deep introspection. What does this helmet look or feel like? Imagine that this will safely transport you into your subconscious, without the fear of losing yourself there.

goddess analysis

6

In the same way that our astrological charts are more than our Sun signs and contain a variety of elements that all contribute to our unique personalities, so a variety of Goddess energies resides in us all. Some are dominant throughout our lives and thus are highly recognizable. I have always known about the Athena in me and this has been most obvious in the way I have acted as champion to the men in my life, taking pleasure in orchestrating their careers and being the "power behind the throne."

Demeter never seemed to be an archetype I could relate to, but she has been lying dormant all these years. It was not until 6,000 miles separated me from my teenage children and I yearned for their company that I could finally acknowledge her. And I have a sneaking suspicion that I will learn to grow old disgracefully and embrace Kali Ma and the Cailleach now that I am living near San Francisco, California, and am

being forced to reassess, challenge, and shake off some of the judgmental, intolerant, and narrow-minded attitudes I grew up with.

You may have found, as you read the Goddess stories, that a number resonate strongly with you, either because you recognize and delight in those qualities now or wish to develop or modify them in the future. I had always wanted to be more like Artemis and am working on developing her independent, adventurous, and self-reliant spirit, but within a relationship rather than outside one. Just be aware that, despite being categorized as Maiden, Mother, and Wise Woman, these Goddesses will not necessarily appear in chronological order. I know a number of middle-aged Persephones, Demeters who are barely in their teens, and Hecates who have developed unusual intuition and wisdom despite only being in their twenties or early thirties.

The following charts have been devised to help you better understand how different Goddesses can manifest themselves in your life at particular times and how each of them contains the potential for both functional and dysfunctional qualities. I hope that they also serve as resources for helping you discover more about yourself, your core values, and the qualities you need to develop or downplay in order to live a happier and more fulfilled life.

In writing this book I have been forced to focus on many issues of my own, particularly menopause. I have discovered, for example, that the word "crone" may have originated from "crown," that universal symbol of regalness. For me it is time to push aside the trappings of a princess and accept the mantle of a queen. What transformation is it time for you to embrace?

It is said that we are living in the age of information. But information alone does not bring you closer to truth, wisdom, or happiness. One of the most effective ways of achieving enlightenment is to respond positively to everything that comes your way; to live life with a resounding "YES!!!" Therefore I encourage you to welcome each and every goddess whose power and energy is made apparent in your life, regardless of how appealing or relevant she may seem to you now. Each goddess has something to teach you about yourself. It is having greater knowledge of the Self that causes wisdom to grow and it is self-mastery that is true power. Reflecting on various life events in relation to the goddess mythologies can help you to identify which attitudes, beliefs, and behavior you have historically embraced that may no longer be relevant or appropriate to your current life. The following pages highlight nine such circumstances, although not all of these will necessarily be relevant to you at the present. Their purpose is to prompt you to meditate on specific questions or issues and suggest one Goddess archetype to explore further, one that

has a specific relationship to that particular life event. There is no conclusion to an exercise such as this. It is merely a tool by which you can further explore how much of your story is outmoded and needs to be rewritten or modified. I hope it will also offer you some insights into how you might more easily make the most of the rites of passage yet to come.

birth

✳ **Questions:** What was the nature of your birth experience? Did you come into what you perceived as a child as a loving, welcoming world, or a cold, fear-filled climate of abandonment? How has that informed the way you see the world today? To what extent are you setting up a self-fulfilling prophesy?

Athena's dramatic "birth" from the head of Zeus serves to eliminate her mother, Metis', role not only in this event but also throughout her life (see pp. 64–65). Athena thereafter was her father's trusted confidante and her entire way of being was more typically masculine than feminine. A renowned strategist, Athena's story focuses on war and patriarchal values.

✳ **Key issue:** Many of us have a tendency, from the moment we are born, to feel more connected with one parent than the other. Think about how true this is for you. If, like Athena, you related more to your father than to your mother as a child, consider how far you may be denying your feminine nature in order to be more like your idol. Does logic always win out over intuition, for example? And, by living constantly in your head, are you missing out on the essential experience of connecting with your body?

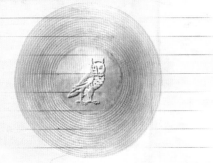

birth of siblings

✳ **Questions:** What age were you when your siblings were born? What were your early relationships with them like and how have these been maintained or changed over the years? Did you experience feelings of jealousy, companionship, rivalry, or perhaps even disinterest, toward your brothers and sisters?

Artemis (see pp. 46–51) had a twin brother, Apollo – the Sun God to her Moon deity. In many ways the two opposites are complementary, as is the nature of Yin and Yang. He was most at home in the cities, while she made her domain in the wilderness and in Nature. Apollo was said to be the protector of domestic animals, while Artemis' flock contained the wild and untamed. Artemis is also noted for her sisterly relationship with the many nymphs who acted as her companions.

✳ **Key issue:** In some cases the nature of your relationship with siblings colors one's relationship with nonfamily males and females, since it is in the home that we first learn how to become social beings. Have you always sought out lovers who remind you of your brother(s), and treat them as such, as Artemis did? Does your attitude to female friendships suffer or benefit from your relationship with your sister(s)?

puberty

* **Questions:** How fully prepared were you, by your parent or caregiver, for the physical, emotional, and psychological changes of puberty? Were the messages you received about your physical and sexual development positive, negative, or nonexistent?

Persephone (see pp.56–61), the Maiden Goddess, could only achieve her power, both as a woman and as a unique being, with a mission to fulfill once she had been separated from her mother. From that loss emerged the equality that every daughter must experience in her relationship with her mother. This enriches the lives of both, since there is a sharing of knowledge that a mother can give only when her child has also become a sexual and reproductive being. Until that time their relationship is only partial.

* **Key issue:** Reflect on your current attitude toward your body and your sexuality. How comfortable are you with these two aspects of yourself? Then consider the extent to which your attitudes have been influenced by your experience during puberty. Remember that you are no longer a confused, uninformed teenager, but a woman who can change her attitude about herself anytime she chooses.

marriage

＊ **Questions:** Why did you decide to get married? What influences, apart from "love," may have played a part – getting away
from your parents, financial security, low self-esteem, a desire for
status? How much spiritual connection did/do you feel you have
with your partner?

Kwan Yin's story (see pp. 52–55) is typical of the pressure extended to young women to get married. In her case it was intended
that the union should bring greater wealth and status to her
father's household. Even today, in some families, women endure
scathing comments about being "left on the shelf," being "too
choosy," or "putting men off," by family members who are
merely projecting their own insecurities onto them.

＊ **Key issue:** Consider the balance between the internal (from the
Self) and external (from others) pressures that had an impact on
your decision to marry. Is this the best life state in which to make
such an important choice? Reflect on what might be the most
enlightened influential factors.

motherhood

✳ **Questions:** What does the term "motherhood" mean to you? How are you rebelling against the circumstances of your own childhood in the way that you are choosing to bring up your own children?

Gaia (see pp. 90–91) is the archetypal Mother Goddess, the creator and nurturer of the world, a generous deity, from whom all things are brought into being. Mother Nature, or Gaia, represents a delicately balanced, interdependent ecosystem, in which all things depend on each other for survival, in particular, the continuing existence of the human race and all living creatures on planet Earth rely on the health and well-being of Gaia. Thanks to environmental groups, humankind is beginning to learn that it cannot continue to rape and plunder the resources of this planet, but must learn to work in harmony with Nature in order to share her bountiful resources. Similarly, human mothers need to ensure that they get back as much as they give out, by learning to nurture and care for themselves physically, emotionally, and spiritually.

✳ **Key issue:** Think of all the ways in which you deny your own wants and needs at the expense of your role as a mother. If you accept that the Universe is abundant in its love and all other resources, is it not possible to give to yourself without denying or reducing your maternal generosity?

infidelity/divorce

* **Questions:** What is your perspective on fidelity? How important is it to you that you and your partner remain faithful to each other? Is this a core value for you? Under what circumstances, if any, do you believe that your attitude to this might change?

  Hera (see pp. 84–89) endured many years of humiliation and betrayal at the hands of her feckless husband, Zeus. Eventually, she summoned up the courage and self-esteem to leave him and steer her own course. It was only when she learned to "let it be" and accept that there was nothing she could do to change him, only change herself and her attitude toward his behavior, that Hera achieved a sense of inner peace. Ironically, it was then that Zeus became anxious to get his wife back, and, pretending to marry what turned out to be a lifeless statue, demonstrated that all his extramarital entanglements had been lifeless and unimportant in the great scheme of things, compared with his union with Hera.

* **Key issue:** If your partner is continually unfaithful or humiliates you by flirting with others, consider the extent to which you are unfaithful to your core values. Could it not be argued that you are conspiring in your own humiliation by putting up with his errant behavior? Or are you blaming other women – as Hera did, rather than telling it like it is and laying the responsibility for your partner's actions squarely on his shoulders? We are often afraid of articulating our values, even to loved ones, particularly when we think that there is a risk that they will leave us because they do not share them. What vitally important values have you neglected to express to your partner – and why?

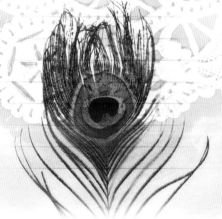

children leaving home

* **Questions:** What emotions do you experience when you think about your children growing up and leaving home? How might your fears about this event be forming, even subconsciously, the attitudes and behavior you are exposing your children to? Why are you holding them responsible for your future happiness?

  Demeter (see pp. 78–83) is the archetypal "empty-nester," a woman who will do anything to keep her daughter a child in order that she herself is not "abandoned." This archetype fosters dependency in her children through a variety of dysfunctional behaviors. These include insisting that they always tell her where they are and who they are with, even when this is inappropriate, and making them feel guilty if they fail to do exactly as "Mommy" tells them. This is the mother who treats her grown-up offspring as if they were still children who need her support and guidance for their survival and well-being.

* **Key issue:** Think about one ambition that you put on hold when you took on the role of caregiver to your partner and children. Could it be that you are gripping your children tightly to you because you are fearful of taking on another role that you perceive as somehow riskier, such as returning to work? How might you begin to make that earlier dream a reality now that you are more mature, experienced, wiser, and free?

menopause

✳ **Questions:** How do you feel about aging – not in some theo-
retical, objective sense, but in respect to your own body, life, and
perceived value in society? What are you most afraid of?

Cailleach (see pp. 104–109) is just one example of the third age
of the Goddess – the Wise Woman, Witch, or Crone. Menopause
is a time when the fact that they are aging is really hammered
home to women. Only the enlightened few welcome this stage
in their lives, recognizing it as freedom, not just from menstruation and pregnancy, but from the slavery of patriarchal values of
beauty. This inspiring Goddess judged herself by her own values
and was said to have maintained a vigorous sex life with men
much younger than herself, who eventually died of old age while
she remained ageless.

✳ **Key issue:** Think carefully about what limitations you are placing on yourself at this time in your life. Consider what exactly you
have lost from going through menopause. How much of it is really important? Inspire yourself by reading about women whose
creativity and success have come to them late in life, such as
author Mary Wesley, whose first best-selling novel was published
in her late middle age. Counterbalance the frequently negative
messages about the menopause by reading Leslie Kenton's book,
A Passage to Power.

death

* **Question:** To what extent do you fear death, and why? Isis' story (see pp. 72–77) of how she brought her beloved husband and brother, Osiris, back to life, is a wonderful metaphor not only for the power of love but for how this energy force continues to exert its influence on the world, even when those who have loved fully have died. This ancient Egyptian Goddess and her sister, Nephthys, were Queens of the Dead, searching relentlessly for the pieces of Osiris' body that his brother, Seth, threw to the four winds. One of Isis' symbols is the ankh, the Egyptian hieroglyph for "life." This reminds us that there is life even in death and that the nature of existence is cyclical, with one stage irrevocably following the other.

* **Key issue:** Make a list of all the legacies that you will leave behind when you die. Does the extent of this list surprise and delight you, or shock you because of its limitations? If the latter, are you being fair to yourself and including all the ways you have had an impact on your family, community, and the world? What might you commit yourself to doing today to ensure that your memory is held in the highest esteem by the widest number of individuals?

The functions and dysfunctions of the nine main Goddesses

This chart lists the nine major Goddesses featured in this book. Use it as a checklist of functional and dysfunctional qualities in your personal growth program. They are listed in alphabetical order.

Goddess	Functional qualities	Dysfunctional qualities
ARTEMIS (pp. 46–51)	Independent Adventurous Self-reliant Nurturing Passionate Free-spirited Protective (of others)	Uncompromising Overly competitive Vengeful Merciless Superior Invulnerable Armored (of self)
CAILLEACH (pp. 104–109)	Inner strength Unmaterialistic High self-esteem Creative Powerful	Manipulative Ruthless Stern/cold Destructive Vindictive
DEMETER (pp. 78–83)	Earth Mother Nurturing Strong maternal instinct Generous Persistent	Overly protective Self-neglecting Narrow thinking Uncompromising Needs to maintain status quo
HECATE (pp. 110–113)	Creative Intuitive Protective Transformative Mentoring	Destructive Ignoring Manipulative Secretive Distant

Goddess	Functional qualities	Dysfunctional qualities
HERA (pp. 84–89)	Regal Powerful Supportive Needs commitment Dedicated homemaker	Jealous Vindictive Quarrelsome Denies partner's faults Puts partner first
ISIS (pp. 72–77)	Persistent Devoted Insightful Resourceful Loyal	Martyr Cannot accept endings Self-sacrificing Devious Mournful
KALI MA (pp. 98–103)	Creative Protective Powergiving Free Tolerant	Destructive Vengeful Devouring Fierce Wild
KWAN YIN (pp. 52–55)	Altruistic Compassionate Unconditional love Fearless Integrity Holding clear values In service to others	Self-sacrificing Unrealistic Rescuing – codependent Lack of life balance None Neglect of Self None
PERSEPHONE (pp. 56–61)	Surrendering Adventurous Balanced Empowered through adversity Recognition of personal power	Dependent Fear of change Depressive/despairing Fails to see positive Passive

claire: the maiden

Claire remembers feeling physically sick when her mother began to discuss menstruation in order to prepare her for the changes about to take place in her body. As a well-developed young girl, she would cringe at having to take her clothes off in her school's communal changing rooms. In class she was deeply embarrassed by the attention her large breasts attracted from male students.

Because of her mature looks, Claire found it easy to date much older boyfriends when she was barely into her teens and she lost her virginity to one of them in order to "prove" her love for him. This trend continued and Claire eventually married a man closer in age to her father (who was away on business for extended periods during Claire formative years) than to herself. She relied on her husband for everything, and friends were concerned about the inequality of the relationship, with Claire acting more like a little girl in his presence than a woman in her mid-twenties.

Before the couple was able to celebrate their tenth wedding anniversary, Claire's husband died. Now a widow barely into her thirties, she was bereft and seemed to have no idea about how to look after herself. Since her husband had paraded her as his trophy wife, Claire had never had to work and had no understanding of how to manage finances or legal affairs. She relied on relatives and friends to help her sort out her life, and she came to lean on them, even for the most trivial of matters, in exactly the same way as she had been encouraged to lean on her husband.

However, a few years later a close friend, irritated at having been woken up by Claire late at night about a relatively minor matter, retorted that now that she was approaching forty wasn't it about time she grew up and started taking responsibility for herself? Claire was informed that other people were getting tired of her constantly playing the role of victim. These catalytic comments shocked Claire into facing up to how dependent on other people, particularly men, she had always been.

That New Year, Claire made a commitment to take charge of her life and signed up for an adult education class in order to learn how to use a computer. She took advantage of a plethora of expert advice on money matters and forced herself to deal with day-to-day problems rather than immediately picking up the telephone to plead with someone else to fix them.

As Claire developed more confidence her self-esteem soared. She completely changed her wardrobe, wearing clothes more suitable for her age group and took greater pleasure in her voluptuous figure. She recently remarried, this time not to a father figure who would force her to remain a little girl, but to a man who truly admired and respected the competent, dynamic woman that she had become.

Claire had been gripped by the inertia of Persephone (see pp. 56–61). Like Peter Pan, she had been afraid of growing up, until it was pointed out to her how inappropriate it was for a woman her age to be so dependent on others. By taking direct action to boost her self-esteem and self-responsibility, Claire learned to suppress the Persephone influence, replacing it with a more appropriate Maiden archetype, such as Athena (see pp. 64–65).

june: the mother

June always knew best. Her favorite phrase was, "Didn't I tell you so?," accompanied by a superior smirk. June liked the fact that she was always right, at least in her own view. The trouble was, this desire to feel important and valuable had, over the years, alienated both her husband and children. The latter, a boy and twin girls with barely 18 months between them in age, all left for college within a short space of time. It was no coincidence that they all chose locations many miles from home.

Despite her attempts at invoking dependency in her children, all three had strong personalities and resented the way their mother seemed to interfere in every aspect of their lives, from making inappropriate remarks about their friends to pouring scorn on their fashion sense. Little did June realize that her desire to involve herself totally with her children was the very thing that drove them away.

June had always put the children first. She had longed for a bigger family, but after two miscarriages following the birth of the twins she had been advised to give up trying for more children. June, who had never had a particularly strong sex drive, shunned marital relations soon afterward, there no longer seemed any point. She suspected that her husband had had the occasional fling, but she was too caught up with the children to care. Her life was fulfilled and full.

Now June and her husband were strangers and within six months of the children leaving home he too packed his bags and went to live with his long-time mistress. June was beside herself and considered her life to be without purpose. A close friend, concerned that she might do something silly, suggested that June see a counselor to discuss how she might climb out of the pit of despair she found herself in. The psychotherapist June visited helped her rediscover layers of half-remembered passions that had become buried under years of putting other people's needs first. June knew that she did not want to return to paid work and was grateful that her husband continued to pay the mortgage and help out with other expenses, to assuage his guilt at his leaving. Several insurance policies had matured, providing June with a sizeable income.

An avid reader, June immersed herself in books, took a number of literature courses, and joined various local reading groups, where she made new friends. With the help of her psychotherapist, June recognized her tendency to act like a mother hen to younger members of these various groups and made a concerted effort to counterbalance this desire to mother others by being a good mother to herself. Since focusing more on her own life, June has found that her children are eager to visit her more often. She just needs to remember to let them make their own choices and their own mistakes and that there is a fine line between a nurturing mother and one who takes this to the extreme and smothers her young.

June is typical of a strong Demeter archetype (see pp. 78–83), a woman who has so much invested in fostering dependency in her children and is prepared to put her own ambitions on hold in order to do so. In therapy she was encouraged to develop a more empowering archetype, in her case, Gaia (see pp. 90–91), so she could form a more authentic and fulfilling relationship with herself.

laura: the wise woman

For fifty years Laura had lived an inauthentic life, but this was her safety net. She had been brought up in a family where expressions of emotion were punished. If young Laura was angry at an unreasonable demand by a parent or unfair treatment in comparison with a sibling, she learned to suppress it. It was "not done" in that house for children to vent their feelings. Being very emotional, Laura developed a well of unexplored sensitivity that would threaten her mental or physical health. It was not until she approached menopause that Laura found she could no longer hold her feelings in. As she lay in bed, bathed in sweat and fearful of the changes going on in her body, she would be racked with grief and sob until the small hours. Not understanding why she was exhibiting these signs of depression, given that her life was in other ways happy, Laura wondered if she was going slightly mad. Laura had always avoided confrontation. She rationalized this withholding of her true feelings as being kind to others. Instead of telling a friend or colleague that she thought their behavior hurtful, Laura would let it pass so as not to risk an argument. She did not feel safe having arguments. When she had tried to stand up for herself as a child, her mother had beaten her, and this lesson had never left her.

Laura entered a competition and won a vacation for two in the Far East. When she told her best friend about it, the woman automatically assumed that Laura was asking her to go with her and began to talk enthusiastically about what a great time they would have. Laura only stared back. She had never thought of offering the other place to her friend. While they loved each other dearly, they had very different interests and ideas about vacations. Not knowing what to do, Laura let time pass until it got to the point where she had to say something. Not knowing how to handle the situation, Laura confided in a close friend. This was what she heard:

"Stop withholding how you feel, Laura. You are no longer a child but a grown woman. No one is going to beat you because you are speaking the truth. In your heart you have no wish to hurt your friend, so why do you think that she will take the news badly? Trust yourself and your friend. Fear of speaking out is destroying you. There is such wonderful freedom in being open and honest. Take the risk and see what happens. If this person is a true friend she will accept what you say. She may be disappointed and annoyed that you didn't speak up before, but she's not going to end a friendship because of it. Get in touch with your Inner Child: the one that is damaged by your upbringing, and give her the love your mother failed to give you. Remember how children can be honest and no one is offended. Reawaken that side of yourself, and you will find that everything works out fine."

Laura met her friend next day. In a somber tone she began to explain why she did not want to take her on the trip. Her friend looked alarmed and said, "You scared me to death. I wondered what on earth you were about to tell me. Look, this isn't a problem. I'd half guessed that you had plans to take someone else and meant to say I was fine with that, but it slipped my mind." Laura was so relieved that she burst into tears. Her friend then passed on some good advice in the ways of the Wise Woman: "Nothing spoken or done with goodness in the heart is ever bad or hurtful because the recipient doesn't just hear the words but the emotional content behind them. Truth is freedom. And freedom is the ultimate gift of the Wise Woman."

To reinforce this message, Laura attended goddess workshops. She found herself attracting the Kali Ma (see pp. 98–103) and the Cailleach (see pp.104–109) archetypes into her life. Kali Ma helped her realize that changing circumstances require modified ways of thinking and being; the Cailleach demonstrated that true maturity involves the ability to express oneself freely and authentically.

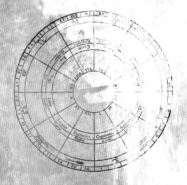

finally I recently received an e-mail from a friend, the sort of thing that people distribute to many others electronically, entitled Beautiful Women. It outlined the various stages in our female lives and the resultant ebb and flow of our self-esteem.

The following is my own, amended, version of this inspiring piece, and I would like to dedicate it to everything that you, as a woman should, will, and can be, as well as what you are. For you are the most amazing, beautiful, and talented woman in the world.

Age 5: When she looks at herself the little girl sees a fairy princess with a whole, magical world out there to discover.

Age 10: When she looks at herself the emergent young woman sees Cinderella or Sleeping Beauty; she's just waiting for the right boy to come along to bring that world to life for her.

Age 15: She prefers not to looks at herself because all she sees is baby fat, pimples, and plainness. She would like to hibernate until she's grown up.

Age 20: She tends to look at pictures of supermodels and compares them to herself, not very favorably.

Age 30: She hasn't the time to look at herself; she's too busy climbing the ladder of success.

Age 40: She hasn't bothered to look at herself too closely lately as she's more interested in being judged by her brains and personality than her looks.

Age 50: She suddenly looks again at herself and becomes concerned about the changes. She begins to mourn the passing years.

Age 60: She thinks: "What the heck. At least I've still got good health and good eyesight so I can still see myself in the mirror." She jumps on her motorcycle and roars off into the distance.

Age 70: She looks at herself and sees the road map of experience outlined on her face and is delighted by this physical manifestation of all the wisdom that life has brought her. She knows that, God willing, she can do just about anything she pleases.

Age 80: She no longer cares about what's on the outside. She puts on a big floppy hat and decides to go out and have some fun.

The Goddess discovered Life is there for experiencing and learning in our own individual ways. It is up to each one of us to seize every opportunity as it comes along and, having learned what the Goddesses can teach us at different life stages, pass on our wisdom to others.

further reading

Bolen, Jean Shinoda. *Goddesses in Everywoman: A new psychology of women*. HarperPerennial, 1984.

Conway, D.J. *Maiden, Mother, Crone: The Myth and Reality of the Triple Goddess*. Llewellyn Publications, 1999.

Dunn Mascetti, Manuela. *Goddesses: An Illustrated journey into the myths, symbols and rituals of the Goddess*, Barnes and Noble, 1998

Goodison, Lucy and Morris, Christine (eds), *Ancient Goddesses*. British Museum Press, 1998.

McLean, Adam. *The Triple Goddess: An exploration of the Archetypal Feminine*. Phanes Press, 1989

Monaghan, Patricia. *The Goddess Path: Myths, Invocations and Rituals*. Llewellyn Publications, 1999.

Osho. *The Book of Wisdom*. Element Books, 2000.

Simpson, Liz. *The Book of Crystal Healing*. Sterling Publishing Co. Inc., 1997.

Simpson, Liz. *The Book of Chakra Healing*. Sterling Publishing Co. Inc., 1999.

Simpson, Liz. *The Healing Energies of Earth*. Journey Editions, 2000.

Stassinopoulos, Agapi. *Conversations with the Goddesses: Revealing the Divine Power Within You*. Stewart, Tabori and Chang, 1999.

The New Larousse Encyclopedia of Mythology, Hamlyn Publishing, 1959.

Waldherr, Kris. *Embracing the Goddess Within: A Creative Guide for Women*. Beyond Words Publishing, 1997.

Walker, Barbara G.*The Woman's Encyclopedia of Myths and Secrets*. HarperSanFrancisco, 1983.

Woolger, Jennifer Barker and Woolger, Roger J. *The Goddess Within: A guide to the eternal myths that shape women's lives*. Fawcett Columbine, 1987.

resources

Just typing the word "goddess" into the Google searchengine (www.google.com) revealed 19,100 web sites on the subject. Not all of them offer workshops, conferences, retreats or other events, but many do. Inputting the name of a particular goddess of interest to you, or the words "maiden", "mother", "wise woman" or "crone" will undoubtedly reveal many more. In addition, you may find your local healing center or alternative religion center may offer goddess courses, ceremonies, or consultations. As with any program of this kind, do ask plenty of questions before signing up, such as:

* What exactly does the course involve?
* What is the total cost and what does that include?
* Who are the facilitators and what experience do they have?
* In what way is this course likely to benefit me?

Some course facilitators may not necessarily be completely open about what they expect of participants. I recall one weekend workshop that I attended which involved dancing naked in the open air and submerging oneself in an ice-cold pond. Some people may well love this sort of activity, but others may feel uncomfortable about what is being expected of them. It is easy to feel pressure from the group and it may be difficult to opt out once the event is underway.

Readers with access to The Learning Annex (e.g. New York and San Francisco) might like to check www.learningannex.com for speakers on the subject of "the goddess within." Two further US contacts are: Agapi Stassinopoulos, author of Conversations with Goddesses, whose website www.conversationsgoddesses.com/ gives details of her tour dates. And Jennifer and Roger Woolger, authors of The Goddess Within, offer seminars, workshops, lectures and festivals on the goddess and Jungian psychology. They can be contacted through:
Laughing Bear Productions
5 River Road
New Paltz, New York
12561USA

index

Acknowledgments
Gaia Books would like to thank the following for their help in the production of this book: Pip Morgan, Susanna Abbott, and Jinny Johnson for editorial help; Matt Moate for early designs; Elizabeth Wiggans for indexing; Nanette Hoogslag for her beautifully interpreted illustrations, and images for photography on pages 2, 5, 9, 139.

Nanette Hoogslag would like to thank all the goddesses who assisted in the creation of the illustrations, and a special thank you to David.

BOSTON PUBLIC LIBRARY

3 9999 04653 301 2

WITHDRAWN
No longer the property of the
Boston Public Library.
Sale of this material benefits the Library.

Allston Branch Library
300 N. Harvard Street
Allston, MA 02134

BAKER & TAYLOR